Copyright © 2024
All Rights Reserved.

Contents

A Night of Revelation 1

The Call to Connection 4

The Language of Faith 6

Part II: Love as the Foundation 50

Part III: Compassion as the Bridge 67

Part IV: Unity in Diversity 80

Part V: Purpose as a Sacred Gift 95

Part VI: A Shared Journey 112

A Night of Revelation

It began as an ordinary evening. I was alone in a quiet hotel room after a long day, the kind of day that shakes you loose from yourself. I had just returned from a powerful training, one that had left me raw, open, and filled with questions I couldn't quite answer. The facilitator had asked us to journal about an exercise we had just done, to reflect deeply on it, what we carried, and how it shows up in our lives. So I sat down, pen in hand, and began to write.

The first few minutes were simple enough. Thoughts spilled onto the page, messy and unfiltered; fragments about life, death, love, and purpose. But as I kept writing, something shifted. My body felt electric, alive in a way I had never known. My heart pounded as though it wanted to break free from my chest. I was laughing, crying, shaking, all at once. It wasn't just emotion; it was something far greater; something I could feel in every fiber of my being.

And then it happened.

I saw.

At first, it was just a flicker in my mind's eye, like light dancing on water. But it grew, becoming clearer and more vivid than anything I had ever experienced. There was a flow to it, an infinite ocean of blues and light blues, moving and shifting with an otherworldly grace. It was One; alive, vibrant, undeniable. Not a word, not an idea, but a presence. I didn't see it with my eyes, yet it was more real than anything I had ever known.

And then the truth came, not in words but in knowing:

We are One. Past, present, and future are not separate. They are One. Mind, body, and soul are not distinct. They are One. You, me, and everything—all One.

I wrote furiously, barely able to keep up with the clarity pouring through me. My hand moved instinctively, over and over again writing "One"—a capital O joined with a lowercase o. It wasn't deliberate; it just happened, as if the truth was writing itself through me.

Hours passed, though it felt like moments. When I finally set the journal down, I tried to sleep, but the visions didn't stop. I closed my eyes, and the images came.

A father cradling his son, holding the child's head to his heart. The boy looked at me with eyes filled with love, while the father faced away. It wasn't just a picture; it was a feeling—a love so vast, so all-encompassing, it swallowed everything else. Then came laughter, joy, happiness. Voices filled with love echoed in my mind, as though the entire universe was alive with celebration.

And then I saw it: a silver obelisk, in perfect symmetry, its surface gleaming. At each of its three corners, three hands rising upward; hands so vivid, they felt sacred. They reminded me of Michelangelo's Sistine Chapel, but different. The other fingers were closed, and the hands rose together in unity from the three corners, converging at the top where they touched. The moment they met, a brilliant light exploded from the tip, brighter than anything I'd ever seen. It wasn't blinding; it was pure, radiant, alive. And with the light came words:

"Your One Task is to Cure."

The voice was calm, familiar, and loving. It spoke with such clarity and authority that there was no questioning it. It wasn't a command but an invitation—a truth I was being called to live.

"What you've just read is not just a story. It is a moment—one that speaks to all of us. The experience was deeply personal, but the truth it revealed is universal. We are not separate. We are One."

The Call to Connection

For as long as humanity has existed, we have sought connection. We've looked to the stars and seen something greater. We've stood on the edges of oceans, on mountaintops, and in the stillness of quiet nights, feeling a pull that defies explanation. This longing—to belong, to connect, to know—is woven into the fabric of who we are.

Religion, love, and purpose are how we've tried to answer this call. They are the ways we've sought to understand the infinite, to express what cannot be seen, and to connect with something far beyond ourselves. And while these paths may look different, at their core, they all point to the same truth: we are part of something greater.

A Universal Thread

Religion is often seen as a dividing line between us—different names, different rituals, different beliefs. But what if these differences were just languages? What if they were prisms reflecting the same light in different ways? At its heart, every faith is an expression of love, compassion, and purpose—a way to connect to the infinite.

This is the thread that runs through all traditions, all people, all moments. It's the thread of unity, of connection, of One.

This book is an invitation to explore that thread. It is not here to challenge what you believe but to deepen it. It is a journey into the shared truths that bind us together, showing us that no matter how different we may seem, we are all part of the same story.

Love, Compassion, and Purpose: The Call of All Faiths

1. Love as the Essence of Connection

Love is the heartbeat of existence. Every faith teaches it—not as a fleeting feeling, but as the essence of life itself. Love is what connects us to one another, to the divine, and to the infinite.

"Think of a time when you felt loved beyond measure. What did it teach you about connection, about something greater than yourself?"

2. Compassion as Love in Action

Compassion is love in motion. It is the way we reach out to others, bridging divides and healing wounds. Across all traditions, compassion is seen as sacred, a way to embody the divine in our lives.

"How has your faith guided you to show compassion? What would it look like to embody compassion more fully in your daily life?"

3. Purpose as the Path Forward

Faith gives us purpose—a way to live in harmony with the infinite. Whether through service, worship, or discovery, purpose is what calls us forward, turning belief into action.

"What gives your life meaning? How has your faith shaped your understanding of your purpose?"

An Invitation to Begin

The truths revealed in that moment of revelation are not mine alone—they are ours. They belong to all of us, waiting to be seen, felt, and remembered.

As we begin this journey together, carry this thought with you:

We are not separate. We are not divided by borders or beliefs. We are One.

The Language of Faith

Faith, in its many forms, is humanity's way of giving shape to the infinite. It is how we reach toward something beyond ourselves, seeking meaning, connection, and purpose. While the language of faith varies across traditions, the essence remains the same: it is an expression of our longing for the divine.

We begin with Christianity, where love is not only central but foundational. To explore Christianity's language of faith is to explore a love so vast and unconditional that it transcends the limitations of human understanding.

Christianity

In Christianity, love is the essence of God. The Bible proclaims, *"God is love"* (1 John 4:8), making love both the origin and the purpose of all creation. This is not a love confined to fleeting emotions or transactional relationships—it is a love that forgives without hesitation, embraces without condition, and endures without end.

This divine love is often described in three forms:

1. **Agape:** Selfless, unconditional love, often seen as the highest form of love.
2. **Philia:** Brotherly love or deep friendship.
3. **Eros:** Romantic, passionate love.

While all three forms are significant, it is *agape*—unconditional love—that serves as the cornerstone of Christian theology. It is the love that God extends to humanity, the love that Christ embodies, and the love Christians are called to reflect in their lives.

Love as the Greatest Commandment

When asked to name the greatest commandment, Jesus answered:

- *"Love the Lord your God with all your heart, with all your soul, and with all your mind. This is the first and greatest commandment. And the second is like it: Love your neighbor as yourself."* (Matthew 22:37–39)

This dual commandment reveals an interconnected truth: to love God is to love others, and to love others is to reflect divine love. These are not separate acts but one unified expression.

This teaching challenges believers to move beyond superficial love. It is easy to love those who are kind to us, those who share our beliefs or values. But Jesus extends the call further:

- *"But I say to you, love your enemies and pray for those who persecute you."* (Matthew 5:44)

Loving an enemy, forgiving the unforgivable—this is the radical nature of divine love. It is not about merit or reciprocity; it is about seeing the image of God in every person, even those who hurt us.

The Parable of the Prodigal Son: A Story of Divine Love

One of Christianity's most profound illustrations of love is found in the Parable of the Prodigal Son (Luke 15:11–32).

The story begins with a younger son who demands his inheritance from his father, a request that is both audacious and deeply disrespectful. The father grants his request, and the son leaves home, squandering his wealth in reckless living. When famine strikes, the son finds himself destitute, feeding pigs to survive—a task that would have been particularly degrading for a Jewish audience.

In desperation, he decides to return home, rehearsing an apology:

- *"Father, I have sinned against heaven and against you. I am no longer worthy to be called your son; make me like one of your hired servants."* (Luke 15:18–19)

But before the son can even speak these words, his father sees him from a distance and runs to him. The father's embrace is immediate, joyful, and unconditional. He orders a feast to celebrate his son's return, saying:

- *"This son of mine was dead and is alive again; he was lost and is found."* (Luke 15:24)

This parable reveals the heart of divine love—a love that does not hold grudges, does not demand penance, but celebrates the return of the lost. The father's love mirrors God's love for humanity, reminding us that no matter how far we stray, we are always welcomed home.

The Cross: The Ultimate Symbol of Love

At the center of Christianity is the cross, a symbol that embodies both sacrifice and redemption. The crucifixion of Jesus Christ is often described as the ultimate act of love:

- *"Greater love has no one than this: to lay down one's life for one's friends."* (John 15:13)

For Christians, the cross is not a symbol of defeat but of victory—a victory of love over hatred, grace over sin, and life over death. It is through this act of self-giving love that salvation is made possible.

The Apostle Paul captures this truth in his letter to the Romans:

- *"But God demonstrates His own love for us in this: While we were still sinners, Christ died for us."* (Romans 5:8)

This love is radical, undeserved, and transformative. It is a love that extends to all people, regardless of their past, their failures, or their worthiness.

Reflection: How Does Love Show Up in Your Faith?

1. *Think of a time when you felt loved beyond measure—by another person, through prayer, or in a moment of stillness. How did it change you?*
2. *What does your faith teach you about love? How can you embody that love in your daily life—toward friends, strangers, even those who challenge you?*

Hinduism

To speak of *Brahman* is to speak of the infinite. It is to attempt to name that which has no name, to describe that which is beyond description. In Hinduism, Brahman is the ultimate reality—the source, essence, and sustainer of all existence. It is both immanent and transcendent, present in every atom of creation yet beyond all things.

Unlike many traditions that conceive of the divine as a personal being, Hinduism expands the idea of divinity into something boundless. Brahman is not a god to be worshipped but the essence from which gods, humans, nature, and the cosmos arise. It is existence itself, woven into every fiber of life, while remaining untouched by the material world.

Brahman: The Infinite and the Finite

Hindu scriptures often describe Brahman using paradoxes, recognizing that human language is insufficient to capture its full nature. The *Upanishads*, the philosophical texts that form the foundation of Hindu thought, present Brahman as both *nirguna* (without attributes) and *saguna* (with attributes).

As *nirguna*, Brahman is formless, timeless, and beyond comprehension. It is the silent presence that underlies everything, the pure being that exists beyond space and time. The *Brihadaranyaka Upanishad* describes it as:

- *"Neti, neti"* (not this, not that).

This phrase reflects the idea that Brahman cannot be defined by what it is, only by what it is not. It transcends all human concepts, existing beyond dualities like good and evil, light and dark, creator and creation.

Yet, as *saguna*, Brahman takes form. It manifests in ways we can see, touch, and understand. It becomes the deities of the Hindu pantheon, the cycles of nature, the rhythm of life. Through these forms, Brahman allows us to glimpse its infinite nature, offering pathways to connection and understanding.

The Oneness of Brahman and Atman

At the heart of Hinduism lies a profound truth: the individual soul (*Atman*) is not separate from Brahman. What we experience as individuality—the sense of being a distinct self—is an illusion (*maya*). In reality, our true essence is one with the infinite.

This idea is beautifully expressed in the *Chandogya Upanishad*:

- *"Tat Tvam Asi"* (Thou art That).

This phrase reminds us that the divine is not something external or distant. It is within us, woven into the very fabric of our being. The journey of life, according to Hinduism, is to awaken to this truth—to move beyond the illusion of separateness and realize our oneness with Brahman.

The Cycle of Creation, Preservation, and Transformation

To help humans comprehend the vastness of Brahman, Hinduism uses the concept of the *trimurti*—three deities that represent the cyclical nature of existence:

1. **Brahma, the Creator:** The force that brings the universe into being, shaping order from chaos.

2. **Vishnu, the Preserver:** The force that sustains life, maintaining balance and harmony.
3. **Shiva, the Destroyer and Transformer:** The force that dissolves old forms to make way for new creation.

These deities are not separate from Brahman but expressions of its dynamic energy. They illustrate the interconnectedness of life, reminding us that creation, preservation, and transformation are not opposing forces but parts of a unified whole.

The Story of Svetaketu: A Parable of Brahman

The *Chandogya Upanishad* tells the story of Svetaketu, a boy who becomes a symbol of humanity's journey to understand the infinite.

Svetaketu's father sends him to study the sacred texts, and after years of learning, the boy returns home, proud of his knowledge. His father, however, asks him a question that humbles him:

- *"Have you learned that by which the unheard is heard, the unseen is seen, and the unknown is known?"*

Svetaketu admits he has not. His father then begins to teach him the nature of Brahman. Using a series of analogies, he reveals the truth:

- Just as salt dissolved in water becomes invisible but is present everywhere, so too is Brahman—pervading all things, unseen but undeniable.
- Just as rivers flow into the ocean and lose their individual identity, so too do all beings return to Brahman, where individuality dissolves into oneness.

This story is a reminder that the divine is not something we must find—it is something we must realize. Brahman is already present within and around us, waiting to be known.

Paths to Realizing Brahman

Hinduism offers diverse paths to realizing our unity with Brahman, recognizing that individuals connect to the divine in different ways. These paths, collectively known as *yogas*, are not merely physical exercises but spiritual disciplines:

1. Jnana Yoga (Path of Knowledge):

Through study and contemplation, seekers delve into the nature of reality, using reason and meditation to uncover the truth of Brahman. This path is intellectual, requiring rigorous inquiry and reflection.

2. Bhakti Yoga (Path of Devotion):

Surrendering oneself to the divine through love and worship. In this path, the seeker develops a personal relationship with a deity or aspect of Brahman, recognizing it as a reflection of the infinite.

3. Karma Yoga (Path of Action):

Performing selfless actions without attachment to outcomes. By offering one's work as a form of worship, the seeker aligns with the flow of the universe.

4. Raja Yoga (Path of Meditation):

Cultivating inner stillness through meditation and disciplined practice, allowing the seeker to experience Brahman directly.

Each path reflects a different way of engaging with the infinite, offering a unique lens through which to understand and connect with Brahman.

Reflection: Recognizing the Infinite in the Ordinary

- *Think of a moment when you felt connected to something vast—perhaps in nature, silence, or an act of kindness. What did it reveal about your place in the world?*

- *How might your life change if you saw the divine in everything and everyone around you?*

Judaism

Judaism, one of the world's oldest monotheistic religions, offers a profound vision of humanity's relationship with the divine through the concept of *brit*—the covenant. At its core, Judaism is a story of connection, not only between humanity and God but also among people. This covenant is both an agreement and a bond, a sacred commitment that defines not only a way of life but a way of being in the world.

Central to Judaism is the idea of *one God*, a divine presence that is eternal, indivisible, and deeply personal. Judaism's God is described with intentionality and care—a being who creates, loves, commands, and listens. Yet, beneath these descriptions lies a truth that resonates universally: God is One, and all creation is unified in this oneness.

The Covenant: A Sacred Relationship

The idea of the covenant begins with Abraham, the patriarch of Judaism, whose story marks the first explicit moment of divine partnership. In the *Book of Genesis*, God calls to Abraham with a simple yet life-altering command:

- *"Leave your country, your people, and your father's household and go to the land I will show you."* (Genesis 12:1)

Abraham's response is immediate. He leaves everything he knows, trusting in the promise of a God he has never seen but deeply believes in. This moment establishes the first covenant between God and humanity, a sacred bond built on faith and mutual commitment.

God's promise to Abraham is both expansive and deeply personal:

- *"I will make you into a great nation, and I will bless you; I will make your name great, and you will be a blessing."* (Genesis 12:2)

This covenant is not about power or dominance but about purpose. Abraham and his descendants are chosen not to rule but to serve, to be a light unto the nations. The covenant introduces a revolutionary idea: that humanity has a role to play in the divine plan, a responsibility to act with justice, kindness, and humility.

The Giving of the Torah: A Collective Covenant

While the covenant with Abraham is personal, the covenant at Mount Sinai transforms it into something communal. After freeing the Israelites from slavery in Egypt, God brings them to Mount Sinai to seal a new covenant:

- *"Now if you obey me fully and keep my covenant, then out of all nations you will be my treasured possession."* (Exodus 19:5)

This moment is monumental. It is here that the Torah—the central text of Judaism—is given, containing not only the Ten Commandments but also a comprehensive guide to living a life aligned with divine will.

The covenant at Sinai is unique in that it is not imposed; it is accepted. The Israelites respond with a powerful declaration:

- *"All that the Lord has spoken, we will do."* (Exodus 19:8)

This acceptance marks a profound moment of unity, as an entire people commit themselves to a shared purpose: to live as partners with God, to bring holiness into the world through their actions.

God's Oneness: The Shema Prayer

The *Shema* prayer, recited daily by observant Jews, captures the essence of Judaism's monotheistic vision:

- *"Hear, O Israel: The Lord our God, the Lord is One."* (Deuteronomy 6:4)

This declaration of God's oneness is not merely a statement of faith; it is a call to action. To recognize God as One is to recognize the interconnectedness of all creation. It is a reminder that there is no division between the sacred and the ordinary, between worship and daily life.

The *Shema* also emphasizes love as central to the covenant:

- *"Love the Lord your God with all your heart and with all your soul and with all your strength."* (Deuteronomy 6:5)

This love is not passive; it is active, expressed through obedience, kindness, and the pursuit of justice.

Justice, Mercy, and Walking Humbly

The covenant is not only about faith but also about action. The *Prophets* repeatedly call the people back to their responsibilities under the covenant, emphasizing that true worship is inseparable from justice and compassion:

- *"He has shown you, O mortal, what is good. And what does the Lord require of you? To act justly and to love mercy and to walk humbly with your God."* (Micah 6:8)

This verse encapsulates the ethical heart of Judaism. The covenant is not fulfilled through rituals alone but through how one lives—by treating others with dignity, defending the vulnerable, and seeking peace.

The Binding of Isaac: A Test of Faith and Love

One of the most challenging stories in Judaism is the *Akeidah*, the Binding of Isaac (Genesis 22). In this narrative, God commands Abraham to sacrifice his beloved son, Isaac, only to intervene at the last moment, sparing the boy.

This story raises profound questions about faith, obedience, and the nature of God. While interpretations vary, one enduring lesson is the depth of Abraham's trust in the covenant. It also reflects the covenant's central paradox: a relationship with the divine demands both love and surrender, both action and trust.

Reflection: Living the Covenant

1. *Think of a time when you felt called to something greater—a moment when you sensed a responsibility beyond yourself. How did you respond?*
2. *What commitments shape your life? How do they reflect your values, your beliefs, and your relationship with the divine?*

Symbols of the Covenant: A Reminder of Connection

Judaism is rich with symbols that embody the covenant, serving as tangible reminders of the divine relationship:

- **The Sabbath (Shabbat):** A day of rest and spiritual renewal, reflecting God's rest after creation and the covenant's call to holiness.
- **The Mezuzah:** A small scroll placed on doorposts, inscribed with the words of the *Shema*, reminding believers to carry the covenant into their daily lives.
- **The Star of David (Magen David):** A symbol of protection and identity, representing God's promise to sustain and protect the Jewish people.

These symbols are not mere rituals; they are living expressions of faith, anchoring the divine connection in the rhythms of everyday life.

Connecting Judaism to the Universal Thread

The covenant is both unique to Judaism and universally resonant. It speaks to a relationship built on trust, love, and mutual responsibility. The oneness of God, central to the *Shema*, echoes a truth found across faiths: that all of creation is interconnected, unified in the divine.

Islam

Islam, one of the world's major monotheistic religions, revolves around the concept of *Tawhid*, the oneness of Allah. At its heart, *Tawhid* is not simply a belief in one God but an all-encompassing principle that defines the essence of existence, humanity's relationship with the divine, and the nature of the universe itself. It is a declaration that Allah is unique, eternal, and incomparable, the source of all that is seen and unseen.

In Islam, *Tawhid* is the foundation upon which all other teachings rest. It is not just a theological assertion but a way of life, guiding how Muslims think, act, and see their place in the world.

Tawhid: The Core of Faith

The central creed of Islam, the *Shahada*, expresses the essence of *Tawhid*:

- *"There is no god but Allah, and Muhammad is His messenger."*

This simple yet profound statement is the entry point to the Islamic faith. It affirms that Allah alone is worthy of worship, rejecting any form of idolatry or polytheism (*shirk*). Allah is described as eternal and uncreated, the originator of all things. The Qur'an declares:

- *"He is Allah, the One; Allah, the Eternal Refuge. He neither begets nor is born, nor is there to Him any equivalent."* (Surah Al-Ikhlas 112:1–4)

This passage encapsulates the unique nature of Allah—absolute, transcendent, and beyond human comprehension.

Unity in Creation: Allah as the Sustainer

Islam teaches that Allah is not only the creator but also the sustainer of the universe. Every atom, every star, every life is a reflection of Allah's will and power. The Qur'an describes Allah's intimate connection with creation:

- *"We created man, and We know what his soul whispers to him; and We are closer to him than his jugular vein."* (Surah Qaf 50:16)

This verse emphasizes Allah's immanence—His closeness to humanity—and serves as a reminder that the divine is present in every aspect of existence. Yet, Allah's immanence does not diminish His transcendence. He remains beyond all that He has created, incomparable and limitless.

The Names of Allah: Reflections of Oneness

In Islam, Allah is known by 99 beautiful names (*Asma'ul Husna*), each reflecting a different aspect of His essence. These names, such as *Ar-Rahman* (The Most Merciful), *Al-Hakim* (The All-Wise), and *Al-Wadud* (The Loving), offer glimpses into the infinite nature of Allah.

Together, these names paint a picture of a God who is both majestic and compassionate, powerful and loving. They invite believers to reflect on the many ways Allah's presence manifests in their lives, fostering a deeper connection to the divine.

Submission and Worship: Living Tawhid

The word *Islam* itself means "submission," reflecting the core principle of living in harmony with Allah's will. For Muslims, this submission is an act of love and trust, a recognition that Allah's wisdom is greater than human understanding.

Worship (*ibadah*) is both a reflection of *Tawhid* and a way to cultivate it. The five daily prayers (*salah*), fasting during Ramadan, giving charity (*zakat*), and pilgrimage to Mecca (*hajj*) are not mere rituals but acts that realign the believer with Allah's oneness.

These practices serve as constant reminders of *Tawhid*, reinforcing the connection between the individual, the community, and the divine.

The Story of Bilal ibn Rabah: A Testament to Faith in Tawhid

One of the most powerful stories in Islamic history is that of Bilal ibn Rabah, an early follower of the Prophet Muhammad and the first *muezzin* (caller to prayer). Bilal was a slave of African descent who embraced Islam at great personal cost.

When his master learned of his conversion, Bilal was tortured in an attempt to force him to renounce his faith. Yet, despite the suffering, Bilal refused to deny Allah's oneness. He repeated a single word:

- *"Ahad, Ahad"* (One, One).

This unwavering declaration of *Tawhid* became a symbol of resilience and devotion. Bilal's story is a reminder that the belief in Allah's oneness is not just a theological concept but a source of strength and liberation.

Tawhid and Human Unity

Tawhid does not only refer to the oneness of Allah but also implies the unity of humanity. Islam teaches that all people are equal before Allah, regardless of race, wealth, or social status. The Prophet Muhammad emphasized this in his farewell sermon:

- *"O people, your Lord is One, and your father is one. There is no superiority of an Arab over a non-Arab, or of a non-Arab over an Arab; neither white over black nor black over white, except by righteousness."*

This message resonates deeply with the universal truth of unity, reminding us that the divisions we create are human constructs, not divine realities.

Reflection: Aligning with Tawhid

1. *Reflect on a moment when you felt deeply connected to something greater. How did it shape your understanding of the world and your place within it?*

2. *What does it mean to see unity in diversity—to recognize that all people, all things, are part of the same divine plan?*
3. *How might your daily actions reflect the principle of oneness in your relationships, your work, and your faith?*

Symbols of Tawhid: The Kaaba

The Kaaba, located in Mecca, is one of the most powerful symbols of *Tawhid*. It is not an object of worship but a focal point for Muslim prayer, a symbol of Allah's oneness and humanity's unity.

During the *hajj*, millions of Muslims from around the world gather around the Kaaba, moving in unison as a testament to *Tawhid*. This act transcends language, nationality, and culture, illustrating the harmony that arises when humanity aligns with the oneness of Allah.

Connecting Islam to the Universal Thread

Islam's emphasis on *Tawhid* echoes a truth that resonates across all faiths: that there is a unity underlying all existence. This oneness is not just a theological principle but a way of seeing the world, of living with love, compassion, and humility.

Buddhism

Buddhism, founded over 2,500 years ago by Siddhartha Gautama (the Buddha), is a path to enlightenment rooted in understanding the interconnectedness of all things. At its heart, Buddhism is not about worshipping a deity but about cultivating insight, compassion, and inner peace. The teachings of Buddhism reveal that suffering arises from the illusion of separateness and that freedom is found through realizing the deep interdependence of all life.

Dependent Origination: The Web of Life

A central teaching of Buddhism is *pratityasamutpada*, or dependent origination, which describes the interconnected nature of existence. This concept asserts that everything arises in dependence upon other factors; nothing exists independently or in isolation.

The Buddha taught:

- *"When this exists, that arises; when this ceases, that ceases."*

This principle is illustrated through the *Twelve Links of Dependent Origination*, which explain how suffering arises and how it can be overcome. It demonstrates that our thoughts, actions, and even identities are shaped by countless conditions, forming an intricate web of cause and effect.

The Four Noble Truths: A Path to Connection

Buddhism begins with an honest acknowledgment of suffering (*dukkha*), not as a means of despair but as a way to open the door to liberation. The Buddha's *Four Noble Truths* lay the foundation for understanding this:

1. **The Truth of Suffering:** Life contains suffering—birth, aging, illness, and death are inherent to existence.
2. **The Truth of the Cause of Suffering:** Suffering arises from craving and attachment, which create the illusion of separateness.
3. **The Truth of the Cessation of Suffering:** Liberation is possible when craving and attachment are relinquished.
4. **The Truth of the Path to the Cessation of Suffering:** The *Eightfold Path* offers a practical guide to ending suffering and realizing interconnectedness.

The Eightfold Path: Living in Harmony

The *Eightfold Path* is a framework for ethical living, mental cultivation, and wisdom. It leads to awakening by aligning our thoughts, actions, and awareness with the truth of interconnectedness.

The path consists of three main areas of practice:

1. **Wisdom:**
   - Right View: Understanding the nature of reality and interconnectedness.
   - Right Intention: Cultivating compassion and renouncing harmful desires.

2. **Ethical Conduct:**
   - Right Speech: Speaking truthfully and kindly.
   - Right Action: Acting in ways that do no harm.
   - Right Livelihood: Earning a living in alignment with ethical principles.

3. **Mental Discipline:**
   - Right Effort: Striving to cultivate wholesome states of mind.
   - Right Mindfulness: Being fully present and aware of the moment.
   - Right Concentration: Developing deep states of meditative focus.

Through the *Eightfold Path*, individuals break free from the illusion of separateness and awaken to the profound interdependence of all things.

The Metaphor of Indra's Net

An ancient Buddhist metaphor captures the beauty of interconnectedness: *Indra's Net*. Imagine an infinite net stretching across the cosmos, with a jewel at each intersection. Each jewel reflects every other jewel in the net, symbolizing the way all things are interconnected and mutually influencing.

This metaphor teaches that every action we take, no matter how small, ripples outward, affecting the entire web of existence. It invites us to live with mindfulness and compassion, knowing that our lives are deeply intertwined with those of others.

Compassion as the Heart of Interconnectedness

Compassion (*karuna*) is a central practice in Buddhism, arising naturally when we understand the interdependence of all beings. If suffering is shared, then easing the suffering of another eases our own.

The Buddha taught:

- *"If you want others to be happy, practice compassion. If you want to be happy, practice compassion."*

Compassion is not only an emotional response but a call to action. It is expressed through small acts of kindness, generosity, and forgiveness, each of which strengthens the bonds that connect us.

The Bodhisattva Ideal: Choosing Unity Over Liberation

In Mahayana Buddhism, the *bodhisattva* represents the ultimate expression of compassion and interconnectedness. A bodhisattva is one who has attained enlightenment but chooses to remain in the world to help others achieve liberation.

This selfless commitment reflects the understanding that individual liberation is incomplete without the liberation of all beings. The bodhisattva vow declares:

- *"However innumerable beings are, I vow to save them all."*

This ideal reminds us that true freedom is found not in separation but in unity.

The Parable of the Mustard Seed: A Lesson in Shared Humanity

One of Buddhism's most poignant stories is the *Parable of the Mustard Seed*. A grieving mother, Kisa Gotami, comes to the Buddha, desperate to bring her dead child back to life. The Buddha tells her to bring him a mustard seed from a household untouched by death.

Kisa searches every home but finds that death has touched every family. Through her journey, she realizes that suffering is universal and that she is not alone. This realization transforms her grief into compassion, allowing her to find peace.

This story teaches that our suffering connects us, and through this connection, we can find healing.

Reflection: Practicing Interconnectedness

1. *Think of a time when you felt deeply connected to another person, nature, or a larger whole. What did it teach you about your place in the world?*
2. *What small action can you take today to ease someone else's suffering? How might this ripple outward?*

Connecting Buddhism to the Universal Thread

Buddhism's teachings on interconnectedness echo a universal truth: that we are not separate from one another or the world around us. By recognizing this unity, we move beyond fear and isolation, living with greater compassion, wisdom, and peace.

Next, we will explore Sikhism, which teaches the oneness of God and humanity through the principle of *Ik Onkar*.

Taoism

Taoism, rooted in ancient Chinese philosophy, offers a profound exploration of harmony and interconnectedness through the concept of the *Tao*. Often translated as "The Way," the Tao is the ultimate principle that governs the universe, the source from which all things arise and to which all things return.

Taoism invites us to align with the Tao, not through force or domination, but through effortless flow. It teaches that unity with the Tao brings harmony, balance, and inner peace, fostering a way of living that is in tune with the rhythms of nature and existence itself.

The Tao: Beyond Words and Understanding

The *Tao Te Ching*, attributed to Laozi, opens with a profound statement:

- *"The Tao that can be spoken is not the eternal Tao. The name that can be named is not the eternal name."*

This paradox highlights the ineffable nature of the Tao. It cannot be fully described or understood; it can only be experienced. The Tao is both the origin of all things and the underlying order of the universe. It is the flow of the cosmos, the principle that connects all life.

While the Tao is universal, its manifestations are infinite. It is the force behind the changing seasons, the cycle of life and death, and the balance of opposites. To live in alignment with the Tao is to embrace the interconnectedness of all things.

Yin and Yang: The Dance of Opposites

One of the most well-known symbols in Taoism is the *yin-yang*, representing the balance of opposites. Yin and yang are not opposing forces but complementary aspects of the same reality:

- **Yin:** The receptive, passive, feminine energy.
- **Yang:** The active, assertive, masculine energy.

The interplay of yin and yang reflects the dynamic balance of life. Day turns to night, chaos gives way to order, and every aspect of existence finds harmony through its relationship with its counterpart.

This concept reminds us that unity is not sameness but the coexistence of differences in harmony. By understanding and embracing this balance, we align with the Tao.

Wu Wei: Effortless Action

At the heart of Taoist practice is *wu wei*, often translated as "effortless action" or "non-action." *Wu wei* is not passivity but a way of acting in accordance with the natural flow of life. It teaches us to let go of resistance, control, and force, allowing the Tao to guide us.

Laozi writes:

- *"The Tao never acts, yet nothing is left undone."*

This principle is seen in nature: rivers flow effortlessly around obstacles, plants grow toward the light without struggle, and the seasons change without human intervention. By practicing *wu wei*, we learn to live with grace and ease, trusting the flow of life to carry us forward.

The Story of the Farmer: A Taoist Parable

A famous Taoist story illustrates the wisdom of non-resistance and accepting life as it comes:

A farmer's horse runs away, and his neighbors sympathize. "Such bad luck!" they say. The farmer replies, "Maybe."

The next day, the horse returns with a herd of wild horses. The neighbors exclaim, "What good fortune!" The farmer says, "Maybe."

Later, the farmer's son tries to ride one of the wild horses, falls, and breaks his leg. The neighbors lament, "Such misfortune!" The farmer responds, "Maybe."

Finally, soldiers come to recruit young men for war but leave the farmer's son behind because of his injury. The neighbors rejoice, "How lucky!" The farmer simply says, "Maybe."

This story reflects the Taoist principle of accepting life's changes without judgment or attachment. What appears good or bad in the moment may later reveal itself to be something else entirely. By flowing with life rather than resisting it, we align with the Tao.

Harmony with Nature

Taoism places great emphasis on living in harmony with nature. The natural world is seen as a reflection of the Tao, offering wisdom to those who observe and emulate it.

Laozi writes:

- *"Nature does not hurry, yet everything is accomplished."*

This principle invites us to slow down, to notice the rhythms of the world around us, and to find peace in simplicity. The Taoist sage does not seek to conquer nature but to learn from it, recognizing that humanity is part of a larger whole.

The Taoist View of Unity

In Taoism, unity is not about conformity but about balance. The Tao connects all things, yet it allows for infinite diversity. A tree does not compete with a river; each fulfills its purpose, contributing to the harmony of the whole.

This perspective teaches us to embrace differences, to see them not as divisions but as necessary parts of the greater pattern. It challenges us to let go of ego and control, finding peace in the interconnected flow of life.

Reflection: Living in Alignment with the Tao

1. Think of a time when you felt "in the flow," where your actions felt natural and effortless. What allowed you to experience this state?
2. Where in your life can you let go of resistance, trusting the natural rhythm of events?
3. How can you embrace the balance of opposites—light and dark, effort and rest, action and stillness—in your daily life?

Connecting Taoism to the Universal Thread

Taoism's teachings on the Tao as the ultimate principle resonate deeply with the universal theme of oneness. The Tao reflects a truth found in all spiritual traditions: that life is interconnected, balanced, and guided by a force greater than ourselves.

Sikhism

Sikhism, founded in the late 15th century by Guru Nanak in the Punjab region of India, is rooted in the belief in *Ik Onkar*, the Oneness of God. This simple yet profound phrase—*Ik Onkar*, meaning "One Creator"—captures the essence of Sikh philosophy. It reflects the unity of all existence and the divine presence in every part of creation.

Sikhism teaches that God is both transcendent and immanent—beyond the physical world yet present within it. By recognizing the oneness of God and humanity, Sikhs strive to live in harmony with each other and with the divine.

Ik Onkar: The Core of Sikhism

The *Mool Mantar*, the foundational verse of the Sikh scripture *Guru Granth Sahib*, begins with *Ik Onkar*:

- *"There is One Creator, Eternal Truth is His Name. He is the Creator, Fearless, Without Hatred, Timeless, Beyond Birth and Death, Self-Existent, Known by the Guru's Grace."*

This verse is a declaration of God's unity and the divine qualities that transcend human understanding. It reminds Sikhs that God is not confined to a specific form or place but is present in all things, from the vastness of the cosmos to the smallest grain of sand.

Equality and Unity in Sikhism

Sikhism places a strong emphasis on equality, grounded in the belief that all humans are created by the same divine force. Guru Nanak declared:

- *"There is no Hindu, there is no Muslim."*

This statement was not a rejection of other religions but a recognition of the underlying unity of all faiths and people. Sikhism teaches that distinctions of caste, race, gender, and religion are human constructs, not divine truths.

This principle of equality is reflected in Sikh practices:

1. **Langar (Community Kitchen):** All people, regardless of background, are welcome to share a meal in Sikh gurdwaras (places of worship), sitting side by side as equals.
2. **Seva (Selfless Service):** Serving others is a core practice in Sikhism, seen as a way to honor the divine within each person.

Love and Devotion: The Path to God

Sikhism emphasizes that the path to God is not through rituals or asceticism but through love, devotion, and remembrance of the divine name (*Naam*

Simran). Sikhs are encouraged to live as householders, finding spirituality in daily life rather than withdrawing from the world.

Guru Nanak taught:

- *"Let the wealth of selfless service be the lasting treasure of your heart; let the remembrance of the Name bring eternal peace."*

This integration of the spiritual and the practical reflects Sikhism's holistic approach to life. Every action, no matter how ordinary, can become an act of worship when performed with love and devotion.

The Role of the Guru: A Guide to Unity

In Sikhism, the term "Guru" refers to a spiritual teacher who brings light to the darkness of ignorance. Guru Nanak and the nine Gurus who succeeded him provided teachings that guide Sikhs toward unity with God and humanity.

The teachings of the Gurus are compiled in the *Guru Granth Sahib*, the Sikh holy scripture. This text is not just a book but is revered as the eternal Guru, providing wisdom and inspiration for generations.

The Khalsa: A Community of Unity and Strength

The *Khalsa*, established by Guru Gobind Singh, is a community of initiated Sikhs who commit to living by the highest spiritual and ethical standards. Members of the Khalsa take five vows, symbolized by the "Five Ks":

1. **Kesh (Uncut Hair)**: A symbol of accepting God's will.
2. **Kangha (Wooden Comb)**: A reminder of cleanliness and order.
3. **Kara (Steel Bracelet)**: A symbol of unity and eternity, with no beginning or end.
4. **Kachera (Cotton Undergarment)**: A sign of self-discipline.
5. **Kirpan (Sword)**: A commitment to protecting others and upholding justice.

The Khalsa embodies the Sikh ideals of courage, compassion, and devotion, serving as a model for living in harmony with the divine and with others.

A Story of Selfless Service: Bhai Kanhaiya

One of the most beloved figures in Sikh history is Bhai Kanhaiya, a Sikh who exemplified *seva* (selfless service) during a time of war.

Bhai Kanhaiya carried water to soldiers wounded on the battlefield, tending to their needs regardless of whether they were friend or foe. When questioned by other Sikhs for helping the enemy, Bhai Kanhaiya replied:

- *"I see no enemies. I see only God's children."*

This story reflects the Sikh belief in the oneness of humanity and the divine, reminding us that compassion knows no boundaries.

Reflection: Living Ik Onkar

1. *Think of a moment when you felt connected to something greater than yourself—a person, a cause, or an experience. How did it change your perspective?*
2. *How can you practice selfless service in your daily life, reflecting the divine presence in others?*
3. *What would it mean to see every person you encounter as a reflection of the Creator?*

Connecting Sikhism to the Universal Thread

The Sikh principle of *Ik Onkar* resonates deeply with the universal truth that all existence is interconnected. It reminds us that beneath our differences lies a shared divine essence, calling us to live with love, compassion, and unity.

Satanism

Satanism is a religion that often elicits strong emotional responses, largely due to misconceptions, media portrayal, and its provocative use of symbols. However, when approached thoughtfully and carefully, we can see that at its core, Satanism—like all belief systems—seeks to address universal questions of individuality, morality, and connection to the greater whole.

To discuss Satanism in this context is not to endorse or reject it but to examine the principles at its heart that align with universal truths: autonomy, self-awareness, and the value of critical thought. By looking beyond its often-misunderstood surface, we can explore the ways in which its teachings, like those of other religions, reflect the search for meaning and purpose. Modern Satanism holds deeply human values that align with universal truths: love for oneself, respect for others, and the pursuit of authenticity and personal growth. Beneath the layers of rebellion and defiance lies a profound recognition of human potential, the transformative power of self-awareness, and a call to live fully and purposefully.

Far from promoting malice or harm, Modern Satanism encourages empowerment, respect for boundaries, and ethical behavior, offering a unique lens through which to explore connection, individuality, and love.

Self-Love and Empowerment: Honoring the Divine Within

Modern Satanism begins with the principle of self-love—not as narcissism but as a foundation for living authentically and responsibly. It teaches that embracing one's strengths, desires, and individuality is an act of honoring the self.

Anton LaVey writes in *The Satanic Bible*:

- *"There is no heaven of glory bright, and no hell where sinners roast. Here and now is our day of torment! Here and now is our day of joy! Here and now is our opportunity!"*

This statement reflects a focus on the present moment, urging individuals to find joy, fulfillment, and meaning in their lives without waiting for an afterlife. In this framework, self-love is a commitment to living fully, treating oneself with the same care and reverence one might extend to others.

Self-love, when understood correctly, becomes the starting point for compassion: when we honor and respect ourselves, we are better equipped to honor and respect others. In finding ourselves, we begin to strip away the ego, beliefs, and perceptions that cloud our true essence. To know oneself deeply is to begin to glimpse the truth of One—a state of unity where individuality and the collective coexist in harmony.

The Golden Rule in a New Light: Respecting Boundaries

Modern Satanism emphasizes consent, respect, and mutual understanding as ethical imperatives. One of the *Eleven Satanic Rules of the Earth* states:

- *"Do not make sexual advances unless you are given the mating signal."*

This rule, though phrased provocatively, underscores a fundamental truth: relationships and interactions must be based on mutual agreement and respect. Far from promoting selfishness, it challenges individuals to act ethically, honoring the autonomy and dignity of others.

Another rule states:

- *"When in another's home, show them respect, or else do not go there."*

This highlights the value of courtesy and consideration, reminding followers that personal empowerment does not excuse disregard for others. In recognizing the boundaries of others, one begins to honor the interconnectedness and unity of humanity.

Rebellion as a Path to Truth and Justice

The figure of Satan in Modern Satanism is not a symbol of evil but of questioning, defiance, and seeking truth. Satan represents the courage to challenge oppressive systems, outdated dogmas, and unjust authority. This rebellion is not about destruction for its own sake but about creating space for individuality, fairness, and progress.

Consider this teaching:

- *"Satan represents vital existence instead of spiritual pipe dreams."*

While it dismisses traditional spiritual aspirations, this statement also encourages followers to focus on what is real, tangible, and impactful. It is a call to engage with the world as it is, to confront challenges head-on, and to contribute to the betterment of society.

This principle resonates with other traditions that value the pursuit of justice and truth. Rebellion, when grounded in love and compassion, becomes a force for positive change.

Love as Authentic Connection

While love in Satanism is often framed in terms of self-love, it extends naturally to others through authenticity and respect. Modern Satanism teaches that genuine relationships are built on honesty and mutual understanding. It challenges followers to discard superficiality and embrace connections that are meaningful and empowering.

As LaVey writes:

- *"Love is one of the most intense emotions felt by man; another is hate. For these two extremes, Satanism represents the middle path."*

This perspective invites followers to explore the depth of their emotions without fear or shame, finding balance and wisdom in their experiences. In embracing love authentically, they honor their humanity and the humanity of others. When the illusions of ego and false perception are stripped away, love becomes the bridge to unity, reflecting the connection between oneself and One.

Compassion Through Self-Awareness

Compassion in Satanism arises not from self-denial but from self-awareness. When individuals recognize their own struggles, fears, and aspirations, they are better able to empathize with others. Modern Satanism encourages followers to act with fairness and to protect the vulnerable, reflecting a deep understanding of the interconnectedness of humanity.

One rule of Modern Satanism states:

- *"Do not harm little children."*

This is not merely a prohibition but a recognition of innocence and vulnerability, reminding followers of their responsibility to protect and nurture those who cannot defend themselves.

In knowing oneself and seeing past one's own illusions, it becomes easier to recognize and honor the shared humanity of others, fostering compassion as a natural expression of love.

Reflection: Living Authentically

1. *How do you balance self-love with compassion for others?*
2. *What beliefs or systems have you challenged in your life, and how has that brought you closer to your own truth?*
3. *How can stripping away ego, preconceived notions, and limiting beliefs bring you closer to knowing yourself and connecting with One?*

4. *What would it mean to love yourself fully, without judgment, and see that love reflected in others?*

Connecting Satanism to the Universal Thread

At its core, Modern Satanism is a call to embrace life with courage, authenticity, and purpose. It teaches that love begins with self-respect and grows outward through ethical action, honesty, and connection. While its language and imagery may seem provocative, its deeper values reflect a universal truth: that each of us has the power to live fully, to love deeply, and to contribute meaningfully to the world around us.

By exploring the misunderstood and often misrepresented aspects of Satanism, we find yet another thread in the tapestry of human faith and philosophy—one that challenges, provokes, and ultimately contributes to the shared journey toward understanding and unity. It reminds us that to find One, we must first find ourselves, stripping away ego, fear, and illusion to uncover the truth of who we are. In this unveiling, we come closer to the divine spark of unity and love that connects us all.

Shinto

Shinto, deeply rooted in Japanese culture, offers a profound and timeless way of understanding the divine through connection with nature. It is not guided by a single sacred scripture but by foundational myths, oral traditions, and living practices. At its heart, Shinto reflects the universal truth that all existence is sacred, interconnected, and alive with spirit.

This absence of centralized scripture makes Shinto unique among religions. Its wisdom is woven into the rhythms of nature, the quiet presence of shrines, and the celebration of life's blessings. It invites us to see divinity not as something distant but as present in the world around us—in the flowing rivers, towering trees, and the gentle breeze that carries whispers of the eternal.

The Kami: The Spirit of All Things

In Shinto, the divine takes the form of *kami*, spiritual presences that inhabit every corner of existence. The *kami* are not gods in the traditional sense but manifestations of life's sacred essence.

- A mountain may house a *kami*, its grandeur inspiring awe and reverence.
- A humble stream may flow with the spirit of a *kami*, nurturing life along its path.
- An extraordinary moment, like the fleeting beauty of cherry blossoms, becomes a reminder of the sacred in the impermanence of life.

The *kami* embody the interconnectedness of all things, calling us to honor the sacredness in ourselves, others, and the world. Through this reverence, Shinto teaches that we are never separate from the divine—we are part of its eternal flow.

Harmony and Gratitude: A Way of Life

Shinto is not a religion of doctrines but a religion of practice, emphasizing purity, harmony, and gratitude. These principles guide followers to live in alignment with the *kami* and the greater whole:

1. **Purity and Renewal:**
   - Rituals of purification (*harae*) cleanse impurities that disrupt harmony, inviting renewal and connection with the divine.
   - Washing hands and mouth before entering a shrine (*temizu*) serves as a simple yet profound act of preparation, aligning the individual with the sacred.

2. **Harmony with Nature:**
   - Shinto teaches that to live in balance with the natural world is to honor the *kami*. Seasonal festivals (*matsuri*) celebrate the cycles of

life and remind us of our place within the greater tapestry of existence.

3. **Gratitude for Life's Blessings:**
   - Through offerings, prayers, and rituals, Shinto fosters a spirit of humility and appreciation. By expressing gratitude, followers strengthen their bond with the *kami*, recognizing that life itself is a gift.

In these practices, Shinto offers a pathway to stripping away ego and illusion, revealing the love and unity that connect us all to One.

The Myths That Guide: Shinto's Foundational Texts

While Shinto lacks a central scripture, its stories and rituals are preserved in foundational texts that provide a window into its philosophy:

- The Kojiki (Records of Ancient Matters):

The myths of the Kojiki narrate the origins of Japan and the deeds of the *kami*, such as Amaterasu, the sun goddess who brings light and life.

- The Nihon Shoki (Chronicles of Japan):

A blend of myth and history, the Nihon Shoki reveals the sacred relationship between the imperial lineage and the *kami*.

- Oral Traditions and Rituals:

Beyond written texts, Shinto's wisdom is lived through rituals like purification, offerings, and festivals. These practices are dynamic expressions of its core values, reminding us that the divine is found in experience, not just words.

Reflection: Embracing Shinto's Wisdom

1. *Think of a moment when you felt deeply connected to nature—perhaps watching a sunrise or standing before an ancient tree. How did it change your perspective on life?*
2. *What simple ritual or practice can you introduce to your daily life to honor the sacredness of the world around you?*
3. *How can living with gratitude, purity, and harmony bring you closer to yourself, others, and the divine?*

Shinto's Contribution to One

Shinto's wisdom lies in its simplicity and depth. It teaches us to honor the sacred in the everyday, to live in harmony with nature, and to approach life with gratitude and humility. While it is deeply rooted in Japanese culture, its principles resonate universally, reminding us that all existence is connected through love and reverence.

Indigenous Spirituality

Indigenous Spirituality encompasses the rich and diverse beliefs, practices, and traditions of Indigenous peoples across the world. Though these traditions vary greatly between cultures, they share a profound reverence for nature and a deep understanding of humanity's interconnectedness with all living things.

For Indigenous peoples, the natural world is not a resource to be controlled but a sacred presence to be honored. This relationship with the earth and its rhythms offers timeless wisdom about living in harmony, respecting life, and embracing the unity of existence—truths that resonate deeply with the essence of One.

Sacred Connections: The Spirit in All Things

A foundational principle in Indigenous Spirituality is the belief that everything in the universe is alive and imbued with spirit:

- Rivers are not just waterways but entities with their own life force.
- Animals are not merely creatures to be hunted but beings with wisdom and lessons to share.
- The earth itself is seen as a mother—nurturing, sustaining, and deserving of care and respect.

This understanding transcends borders. From the Native American belief in the Great Spirit to the Aboriginal Dreamtime stories of Australia, Indigenous Spiritualities around the world recognize that humanity is not separate from nature but an integral part of it.

As the Lakota Sioux teach:

- *"Mitákuye Oyás'iŋ"—All my relations.*

This phrase reflects the unity of all beings, a call to live in harmony and gratitude for the interconnected web of life.

Cycles and Seasons: Living in Balance

Indigenous Spirituality is rooted in observing and honoring the cycles of nature:

- The rising and setting of the sun.
- The phases of the moon.
- The changing seasons and their gifts of growth, harvest, rest, and renewal.

These cycles teach the importance of balance—of giving and receiving, effort and rest, life and death. Ceremonies and rituals, such as the Sun Dance of the Plains tribes or the potlatch gatherings of the Pacific Northwest, celebrate these cycles, fostering connection to the land and community.

The Wisdom of Storytelling

Stories are central to Indigenous Spirituality, serving as a bridge between the human and the divine, the past and the present. Through myths, parables, and songs, Indigenous peoples pass down their understanding of the universe, their history, and their values:

- The Haudenosaunee (Iroquois) tell of the Sky Woman, who fell to Earth and created life on Turtle Island.
- Aboriginal Dreamtime stories describe the creation of the world and its sacred landmarks by ancestral spirits.
- The Hopi speak of Spider Woman, who wove the first humans into being.

These stories are not just entertainment; they are living truths that teach respect for the earth, the importance of community, and the sacredness of existence.

Rituals and Ceremonies: Honoring the Sacred

Indigenous ceremonies are acts of gratitude, connection, and renewal. They honor the spirits of nature, ancestors, and the cosmos. Common practices include:

1. **Smudging:** Burning sacred herbs like sage or cedar to cleanse the mind, body, and spirit.
2. **Sweat Lodges:** Purification rituals that use heat and prayer to foster physical and spiritual renewal.
3. **Vision Quests:** Personal journeys into nature to seek guidance, clarity, or connection with the spirit world.
4. **Offering Rituals:** Giving back to the earth through offerings of food, tobacco, or other sacred items, acknowledging the reciprocity of life.

Each ceremony reflects a shared understanding: that life is a gift, and our role is to live in harmony with all that surrounds us.

Indigenous Ethics: A Blueprint for Unity

Indigenous Spirituality offers a moral framework rooted in respect and responsibility. These ethics are not rules imposed from above but principles that arise naturally from the understanding of interconnectedness:

- **Respect for All Beings:** Treat every living thing as sacred.
- **Stewardship of the Earth:** Care for the land, water, and air, knowing they sustain all life.
- **Community and Sharing:** Prioritize the well-being of the collective over individual gain.

As the Cree prophecy reminds us:

- *"Only when the last tree has been cut down, the last fish caught, and the last river poisoned will we realize we cannot eat money."*

This wisdom calls humanity to return to a path of harmony, humility, and unity with the earth.

Reflection: Listening to the Earth

1. Think of a time when you felt deeply connected to nature—a walk in the forest, the sound of waves, or the stillness of a desert night. What did it teach you about yourself and the world?
2. How can you honor the earth in your daily life, through actions big or small?
3. What stories or traditions from your own heritage speak to the sacredness of the world?

Indigenous Spirituality's Contribution to Ɵne

Indigenous Spirituality teaches that the earth and all its inhabitants are part of a vast, interconnected whole. It reminds us to walk gently, to honor the sacred in all things, and to live with gratitude and humility. These teachings align seamlessly with the universal truth of Ɵne: that life is a web of connection, held together by love and mutual care.

Through its reverence for nature and its recognition of unity, Indigenous Spirituality offers timeless wisdom for a world longing for connection. It invites us to see the divine not as something distant but as present in the earth beneath our feet, the sky above us, and the relationships that sustain us.

Across the many traditions explored—Christianity, Hinduism, Judaism, Islam, Buddhism, Sikhism, Shinto, Indigenous Spirituality, and even misunderstood paths like Modern Satanism—a profound truth emerges: all religions, at their core, seek to answer the same questions. They ask who we are, why we are here, and how we can live in harmony with the world and each other. They strive to connect humanity with something greater—something infinite—while guiding us to foster love, compassion, and unity. In their myriad ways, they provide meaning in a vast, often uncertain world, reminding us that none of us are truly alone in our journey.

Yet, for all that has been explored here, this is just a glimpse into the extraordinary diversity of human belief. The spectrum of faith is as vast as the stars, encompassing countless other religions, sects, and interpretations, each with its own way of seeing, feeling, and expressing the divine. This is not exclusion but a celebration of that diversity—a recognition that every belief, every prayer, every story, is part of the universal song of humanity.

For those whose traditions have not been named here, your faith, your practices, your truths are no less important. They, too, are part of the greater whole, woven into the fabric of existence. They contribute to the symphony of connection and understanding, just as vital as every other thread in this vast, intricate tapestry.

Faith is not a single path but countless rivers flowing into the same ocean. It is a reflection of humanity itself—each tradition shaped by its unique culture, geography, and history yet sharing a common desire to reach for the infinite. Within every faith lies wisdom waiting to be uncovered, a light waiting to be shared. Sacred texts, oral traditions, rituals, and moments of stillness all hold the same yearning: to find meaning, to find peace, to find connection with something greater.

This diversity is not a barrier to understanding; it is a testament to the infinite ways love can be expressed. It shows us that no matter our differences in language, culture, or belief, we are united in our search for truth and purpose. We are united in our hope, in our love, and in our connection to One.

Symbols and Stories as Pathways: Universal Connections Hidden in Plain Sight

Humanity has always used symbols and stories to bridge the gap between the known and the unknown, the tangible and the infinite. Across time and cultures, we have turned to these tools to explain the unexplainable, to connect with the divine, and to find meaning in the chaos of existence. Symbols and stories carry a timeless power. They are not just relics of history but living pathways that guide us toward connection, unity, and the infinite truth of One.

The Eye of Providence: Seeing What Has Always Been

One of the most enduring and enigmatic symbols in human history is the Eye of Providence—a luminous design often depicted as an obelisk or pyramid with rays of light radiating from the top. For many, it is instantly recognizable as the emblem on the back of the U.S. dollar bill. However, its significance stretches far beyond its modern appearance, winding through ancient cultures, esoteric traditions, and spiritual philosophies.

The Eye of Providence has historically represented divine watchfulness—the presence of a higher power guiding and observing humanity. Its roots may trace back to ancient Egypt, where the **Eye of Horus** symbolized protection, healing, and balance. Over centuries, it evolved, appearing in Christian art as an expression of God's omniscience and in Masonic tradition as a beacon of enlightenment and the pursuit of truth.

Yet the true power of this symbol lies not merely in its history but in its resonance. The Eye of Providence—whether envisioned as a pyramid, obelisk, or a glowing point of light—speaks to a universal truth that transcends culture and time. It reflects the culmination of unity, where all paths, thoughts, and energies converge at a single point, illuminating the boundless connection that binds all existence.

The Obelisk and the Convergence of Light

The obelisk or pyramid shape of the Eye of Providence is not incidental. It mirrors a profound spiritual truth: the journey of rising from a broad, divided base to a unified, luminous peak. The pyramid represents the convergence of the many into the One. Its apex, where rays of light emerge, is the point of revelation—where separation dissolves, and enlightenment dawns.

Some may see this light as divine presence, others as ultimate truth, or the infinite love of One. The bright light at the tip represents something greater than the sum of its parts. It is not merely the culmination of understanding but the opening to infinite possibilities, where barriers of ego and illusion fall away, revealing what has always been.

In this moment of union, individuals may hear a voice, feel an overwhelming sense of peace, or experience clarity so profound that it defies explanation. These experiences, though deeply personal, are threads in the same tapestry. They speak to the infinite ways we encounter the divine truth of connection.

The Eye: Vision Beyond Sight

Whether depicted as a literal eye or simply as a radiant light, the "eye" symbolizes something far deeper than observation. It is not about being watched or judged but about awakening to the infinite. It represents vision that goes beyond sight—an invitation to perceive the unity and interconnectedness of all things.

In some traditions, the "eye" may be seen as a symbol of divine presence. In others, it is a representation of inner vision, the ability to see beyond appearances and into the heart of truth. Each interpretation points to the same essence: enlightenment, awareness, and the realization of One.

This symbol reminds us that enlightenment is not a one-size-fits-all experience. Some may see the light; others may hear it. Some may feel it as love, clarity, or purpose. However it manifests, the experience is deeply personal, yet fundamentally the same—a journey to unity, a return to the truth that we are all connected.

Hidden in Plain Sight: The Eye of Providence in Everyday Life

The Eye of Providence also carries a subtle but profound lesson: that truth is often hidden in plain sight. Its placement on the dollar bill, surrounded by phrases like "In God We Trust-One" and *E Pluribus Unum* ("Out of Many, One"), is a reminder that the divine is not distant. It is here, in the everyday, waiting for us to see it with new eyes.

The web-like pattern surrounding the dollar bill is a representation of One, while the phrase *E Pluribus Unum* echoes the ultimate truth of One: that out of many paths, many beings, and many beliefs, there is a single unifying essence.

This symbol does not demand belief; it invites reflection. It asks us to look beyond appearances, to strip away the layers of ego, and to connect with the infinite that resides both within and around us.

The Tree of Life: A Universal Story of Connection

The Tree of Life is another universal symbol, appearing in countless traditions and teachings across the world. Its roots dig deep into the earth, drawing nourishment, while its branches reach toward the heavens, connecting the physical and spiritual realms.

- In **Christianity**, the Tree of Life is a symbol of eternal life, found in the Garden of Eden and promised in the Book of Revelation.
- In **Kabbalah**, the Jewish mystical tradition, the Tree of Life represents the ten *sefirot*—emanations of divine energy that sustain creation.
- In **Norse mythology**, Yggdrasil, the great world tree, connects the nine realms, holding the universe together with its strength and vitality.
- In **Indigenous Spirituality**, trees often symbolize wisdom, community, and the cycle of life. For example, the Haudenosaunee (Iroquois) revere the Tree of Peace, under which warring nations buried their weapons to form a confederacy.

The Tree of Life speaks to something fundamental: the interconnectedness of all things. Its roots remind us of our shared origin, while its branches show us the infinite possibilities of growth and connection. It is a living metaphor for One, uniting us with the earth and the cosmos, with each other and with ourselves.

The Parable of the Blind Men and the Elephant: Understanding Through Unity

A story shared by multiple faiths—including Jainism, Buddhism, Hinduism, and Sufi Islam—the parable of the blind men and the elephant offers profound insight into the nature of truth and connection.

In the story, several blind men each touch a different part of an elephant. One feels the trunk and concludes that an elephant is like a snake. Another touches the leg and says it is like a tree. Another feels the tail and believes it to be like a rope. Each man is convinced of his truth, yet none has the complete picture.

The parable reminds us that our perspectives are limited. Each of us grasps only a piece of the greater whole, shaped by our experiences, beliefs, and perceptions. Only by sharing our insights—by coming together—can we begin to see the full truth.

This story resonates deeply with the essence of One. It challenges us to let go of the need to be "right" and instead to embrace the idea that every perspective holds value. Unity is not about sameness but about bringing our unique pieces together to create something greater.

The Flame as Eternal Light

The flame has long been a symbol of life, hope, and divinity. Its flickering presence evokes warmth and illumination, yet it also reminds us of the fragility and beauty of existence.

- In **Zoroastrianism**, fire is a sacred element, symbolizing truth, purity, and the divine essence.
- In **Christianity**, the flame is often associated with the Holy Spirit, as seen in the tongues of fire at Pentecost.
- In **Hinduism**, the fire of the *yajna* (sacred offering) connects humanity to the divine, carrying prayers to the heavens.
- In **Buddhism**, the flame symbolizes enlightenment, the extinguishing of ignorance through the light of wisdom.

The flame transcends cultural boundaries, embodying the eternal presence of the divine. It reminds us that even in darkness, light persists. It speaks of resilience, connection, and the truth that burns within each of us—a spark of One waiting to ignite.

Symbols and Stories as Mirrors of the Infinite

Symbols and stories are not just artifacts of history; they are living pathways that connect us to the infinite. They transcend language and culture, speaking directly to the soul. Each symbol, whether the Eye of Providence, the Tree of Life, or a simple flame, carries within it a truth waiting to be seen. Each story, whether of creation, unity, or transformation, invites us to reflect on our place in the greater whole.

These symbols and stories remind us that the divine is not confined to distant heavens or ancient texts. It is here, woven into the fabric of our lives, waiting for us to notice, to awaken, and to remember that we are One.

Reflection: The Pathway Within

1. *What symbols in your life have spoken to you, revealing truths that words could not capture?*
2. *Think of a story that has shaped your understanding of the world. How does it connect to the broader truths of love, unity, and connection?*
3. *What would it mean to see these symbols and stories not as relics of the past but as guides for your journey today?*

Part II: Love as the Foundation

Love is the thread that weaves through every tradition, every culture, and every soul. It is the universal truth that transcends words, uniting humanity with the infinite. Across time and faiths, love has been described as divine, eternal, and unconditional—a reflection of the infinite within us and between us. In its purest form, love is not a fleeting emotion but a profound force that heals, connects, and transforms.

At its core, love is the essence of One. It is the language through which the universe speaks, the bond that ties us to each other and to the divine.

1. Love as a Universal Truth

From the sacred texts of the world's religions to the quiet moments of our daily lives, love reveals itself as the highest calling and the deepest truth. It is the foundation upon which all faiths are built, the bridge that connects us to something greater.

Christianity: God is Love

In Christianity, love is not just a virtue but the very essence of God. The Bible declares:

- *"God is love. Whoever lives in love lives in God, and God in them."* (1 John 4:8)

This verse speaks of a love that is unconditional, selfless, and infinite. It is a love that forgives without hesitation, embraces without condition, and endures without end.

The life and teachings of Jesus Christ exemplify this divine love. From healing the sick to forgiving those who crucified him, Jesus showed that love is not passive but active—a force that seeks to uplift, unite, and redeem. His commandment to *"love your neighbor as yourself"* (Matthew 22:39) challenges us to see the divine in others and to act with compassion and grace.

Buddhism: Loving-Kindness and Compassion

In Buddhism, love is expressed as *metta*, or loving-kindness—a boundless, selfless love that extends to all beings. The *Metta Sutta*, a foundational Buddhist text, teaches:

- *"May all beings be happy; may all beings be without disease. May all beings experience the auspicious. May none be subject to suffering."*

This prayer reflects the Buddhist belief in interconnectedness. To love one being is to love all beings, for we are all part of the same web of existence. Compassion (*karuna*), a natural extension of loving-kindness, is the desire to ease the suffering of others, recognizing their pain as our own.

In Buddhism, love is not possessive or conditional. It is a practice, a way of being that seeks to create harmony and joy in the world.

Islam: The Merciful Love of Allah

In Islam, love is a central attribute of Allah, who is described as *Ar-Rahman* (The Most Compassionate) and *Ar-Rahim* (The Most Merciful). The Qur'an frequently reminds believers of Allah's boundless mercy and love:

- *"My mercy encompasses all things."* (Qur'an 7:156)

This divine love is not earned but freely given, a gift that inspires gratitude and humility. Muslims are called to reflect Allah's love in their actions, showing kindness, forgiveness, and care for others.

The Prophet Muhammad exemplified this love through his compassion for the poor, his forgiveness of enemies, and his devotion to the well-being of his community. His teachings remind us that love is not only a feeling but a responsibility—to act with justice, to care for the vulnerable, and to build a world rooted in compassion.

Hinduism: Divine Love as the Path to Liberation

In Hinduism, love is both a human emotion and a divine force that connects the individual soul (*Atman*) with the universal reality (*Brahman*). The Bhagavad Gita teaches:

- *"Whatever you do, whatever you eat, whatever you offer or give away, and whatever austerities you perform—do that as an offering to Me."* (Bhagavad Gita 9:27)

This verse speaks of *bhakti*—devotion to the divine. Bhakti yoga, the path of love and devotion, emphasizes surrendering oneself to God with pure love, free from ego or expectation. Through this love, the devotee experiences unity with the divine, recognizing that all existence is interconnected.

Hindu mythology is rich with stories of love's transformative power, from the devotion of Radha and Krishna to the unwavering commitment of Sita and Rama. These stories remind us that love is a journey that leads to self-discovery and unity with the infinite.

Judaism: Love as Covenant and Commandment

In Judaism, love is both a divine commandment and the foundation of the covenant between God and humanity. The Shema, a central prayer in Jewish tradition, declares:

- *"Love the Lord your God with all your heart, with all your soul, and with all your might."* (Deuteronomy 6:5)

This love is not merely emotional but deeply relational, expressed through action, obedience, and justice. Loving God also means loving others, as reflected in the commandment:

- *"You shall love your neighbor as yourself."* (Leviticus 19:18)

The prophetic tradition in Judaism emphasizes that love must be accompanied by righteousness. As the prophet Micah teaches:

- *"What does the Lord require of you? To act justly, to love mercy, and to walk humbly with your God."* (Micah 6:8)

This union of love and justice reflects the Jewish understanding that love is a force that repairs the world, one act at a time.

Indigenous Spirituality: Love as Respect for All Relations

In Indigenous Spirituality, love is deeply intertwined with respect and reciprocity. The Lakota teaching of *Mitákuye Oyás'iŋ* ("All My Relations") reflects the understanding that all beings—human, animal, plant, and spirit—are connected in a web of life.

Love is expressed through care for the earth, gratitude for its gifts, and reverence for the cycles of life. Ceremonies, such as the Sun Dance or the potlatch, celebrate this interconnectedness, reminding communities that to love one's relations is to love the divine.

Love of Self

Love begins within. To truly love others, to connect with the divine, and to embrace the unity of existence, we must first learn to love ourselves. Self-love is not selfishness; it is the foundation of compassion, the root from which all other love grows. It is the act of seeing oneself as sacred, worthy, and whole—a reflection of the infinite.

The love of self is an invitation to honor our own humanity, to embrace our flaws as well as our strengths, and to treat ourselves with the same kindness and grace we extend to others. It is a practice of gentleness, a stripping away of ego and illusion to uncover the truth of who we are. In loving ourselves, we begin to recognize the divine spark within, the essence of One that connects us all.

The Universal Call to Love Oneself

The love of self is a theme woven through spiritual traditions across the world. Faiths and philosophies teach that to honor the divine, we must honor ourselves:

- **In Christianity**, Jesus links the love of self to the love of others: *"Love your neighbor as yourself."* (Mark 12:31) This commandment assumes that self-love is natural and necessary for loving others authentically.
- **In Buddhism**, self-love is expressed as self-compassion, the recognition that we are deserving of the same care we offer others. The Buddha taught: *"You yourself, as much as anybody in the entire universe, deserve your love and affection."*
- **In Islam**, the Prophet Muhammad said: *"None of you truly believes until he loves for his brother what he loves for himself."* (Sahih al-Bukhari) Implicit in this teaching is the idea that self-respect and self-love are essential for building harmonious relationships.
- **In Hinduism**, the practice of self-love is tied to self-realization. The Upanishads declare: *"Tat Tvam Asi"* (Thou art That), reminding us that to love oneself is to love the divine within.
- **In Indigenous Spirituality**, self-love is seen as part of a balanced life, where caring for oneself ensures one's ability to contribute to the community and honor the natural world.

Stripping Away the Ego to Find True Self-Love

True self-love is not about ego or self-indulgence. It is about peeling back the layers of fear, doubt, and false perceptions to reveal our authentic selves. Ego binds us to illusions of separation, feeding the belief that we are defined by our achievements, possessions, or failures.

To love oneself fully is to let go of these illusions and see the truth of who we are: beings of infinite worth, connected to all things. This process requires patience, courage, and compassion—forgiveness for the times we've judged ourselves too harshly, and gratitude for the journey that has brought us to this moment.

In this journey of self-love, we align with One, recognizing that the love within us is the same love that flows through the universe.

Reflection of Divine Love

Self-love is also a reflection of divine love. To love oneself is to honor the gift of life, the body that carries us, and the spirit that sustains us. It is to see ourselves as worthy of the same grace and compassion we offer others.

The image of a person embracing themselves, holding their own heart with tenderness, is a powerful metaphor for this love. It is not a rejection of others but a realization that by nurturing ourselves, we create the capacity to nurture the world.

Reflection: Nurturing the Love Within

1. *Think of a time when you showed yourself kindness—perhaps by forgiving a mistake, taking rest when you needed it, or offering yourself encouragement. How did it feel to care for yourself in that moment?*
2. *What does your faith teach about self-worth and the love of self? How can those teachings guide you to see yourself as sacred and whole?*
3. *What steps can you take to nurture self-love in your daily life, creating space for healing, growth, and connection?*

The Love of Self as a Path to One

The love of self is not a destination but a pathway. By embracing who we are with kindness and grace, we open ourselves to deeper connections with others and the divine. It is through self-love that we find the courage to love without limits, to see the sacred in others, and to live in harmony with the infinite.

Reflection: Love as Your Foundation

1. *Think of a time when you felt deeply loved—by a parent, a friend, or even a moment of connection with the divine. How did it change you?*
2. *What does your faith teach you about love? How can you embody that love in your daily life?*
3. *How can you extend love to those who are difficult to love, recognizing the divine spark within them?*

A Mother's Love

Love is felt in the quiet, powerful moments that shape our lives. The image of a mother cradling her child, soothing them with her presence, is a profound and universal symbol of divine love. It is a love so deep it defies words—a love that nurtures, sacrifices, and sustains.

A mother's love is tender yet fierce, boundless yet deeply personal. It is the love that stays awake through the night to comfort a crying baby, that gives its all without asking for anything in return. It is a love that holds and releases, that teaches and protects. It is both the embrace that comforts and the push that strengthens, guiding us to become who we are meant to be.

This love is not limited to any one tradition. It is the same love that Christianity calls patient and kind, that Buddhism calls compassionate, that Islam calls merciful, and that Indigenous peoples see in the nurturing earth. It is the love that reminds us we are cared for, seen, and held by something infinite and eternal.

A mother's love is a reflection of the divine's endless care—a reminder that even in our darkest moments, we are never truly alone. It speaks of connection, of unity, of the truth that love, in all its forms, is the essence of life.

A Father's Love

Love is felt in the moments that take our breath away. The image of a father cradling his child, holding them close to his heart, is a profound and universal symbol of divine love. It is a love so vast it swallows everything else—a love that reassures, protects, and unites.

A father's love is a source of strength and guidance. It is the love that carries us when we falter, that stands firm when the world feels unsteady, and that pushes us to grow, even when it means letting us go. It is both the embrace that shelters us and the hand that nudges us forward, teaching us to stand on our own. A father's love is a promise—unspoken but deeply understood—that we are never alone, no matter how far we roam.

This love is not limited to any one tradition. It is the same love that Christianity calls unconditional, that Buddhism calls boundless, that Islam calls merciful, and that Indigenous peoples see in the embrace of the earth. It is the love that reminds us we are cared for, supported, and part of something infinite and eternal.

A Sibling's Love

Love is woven into the bonds we share with those who walk beside us through life. The love between siblings—whether by blood or chosen family—is a profound and complex reflection of connection. It is a love that challenges, supports, and endures. It is the gentle tease that makes you laugh, the quiet strength that lifts you up, and the shared memories that bind you together no matter the distance.

A sibling's love is a mirror and a refuge. It is the love that grows through shared experiences, both joyous and difficult. It is the hand that reaches out to steady you, the voice that speaks truth when you need to hear it most. It is the love that celebrates your victories as if they were its own, that holds space for your pain without judgment.

This love is universal, appearing in the sacred texts and traditions of countless cultures:

- In **Christianity**, the story of Moses and Miriam reflects a sibling's protective love, as Miriam watches over her brother's safety on the Nile.
- In **Hinduism**, the bond between Krishna and his sister Subhadra symbolizes devotion and care.
- In **Islam**, the relationship between Musa (Moses) and Harun (Aaron) demonstrates collaboration and mutual trust.
- In **Indigenous traditions**, the idea of kinship extends beyond family, seeing all members of the community as brothers and sisters, reflecting unity and shared responsibility.

A sibling's love reminds us that connection is not always perfect, but it is enduring. It is the love that grows with us, evolves through the years, and remains a part of us no matter where life takes us. It speaks to the truth of One: that we are not alone, that we are part of something greater, and that the bonds we share are a reflection of the infinite love that connects us all.

A Friend's Love

Love is found in the bonds we choose, in the connection of friendship. A friend's love is a unique and profound reflection of the divine—an act of mutual trust, support, and joy. It is the love that walks with you through life's challenges, celebrates your victories, and holds you in moments of doubt. A friend's love is not bound by obligation but freely given, a reminder that some of the deepest connections are chosen, not inherited.

This love is a partnership of the heart. It is found in shared laughter, in the quiet comfort of presence, and in the understanding that goes beyond words.

A true friend is both a mirror and a guide, showing you the best of yourself while walking beside you as you grow.

Friendship is celebrated in countless traditions and sacred texts:

- **In Christianity**, Jesus says to his disciples: *"Greater love has no one than this: to lay down one's life for one's friends."* (John 15:13) This selfless love exemplifies the depth of friendship as a reflection of divine love.
- **In Islam**, the bond of friendship is seen as a blessing: *"A true believer is a mirror to his brother."* (Sunan Abu Dawood 4918) Friends are called to reflect kindness, honesty, and guidance to one another.
- **In Buddhism**, spiritual friendships (*kalyanamitta*) are seen as essential for enlightenment. The Buddha taught: *"Spiritual friendship is not half the holy life. It is the entire holy life."*
- **In Indigenous traditions**, friendship is woven into the fabric of community, a bond that strengthens the collective and honors the sacredness of relationships.

A friend's love reminds us that we are not alone, even in our darkest moments. It is a love that lifts us up, offering strength when we falter and joy that multiplies when shared. It reflects the truth of One: that connection is not just found in family or faith but in the hearts of those we choose to walk beside us.

The Love of a Husband or Wife

Love is not just an abstract concept; it is lived in the quiet moments, the shared joys, and the challenges that bind two people together. The love between a husband and wife, or two partners in lifelong commitment, is a profound reflection of unity and connection. It is a love that grows through devotion, patience, and the choice to walk life's path together, hand in hand.

This love is both tender and enduring. It is the love that celebrates triumphs and bears the weight of sorrow. It is the love that forgives flaws and embraces imperfection, choosing to see the divine spark in one another even in the face of struggle. It is a partnership that reflects the truth of One: two lives intertwined, supporting and uplifting each other while moving toward a shared purpose.

Sacred Teachings on Marital Love

The love of a spouse is honored and celebrated across spiritual traditions as a bond that mirrors divine love and commitment:

- **In Christianity**, the Apostle Paul writes: *"Husbands, love your wives, just as Christ loved the church and gave himself up for her."* (Ephesians 5:25) This love is not about dominance but about sacrifice, care, and devotion.
- **In Hinduism**, the partnership between Lord Shiva and Parvati symbolizes balance and unity, representing the harmony of opposites in a sacred bond.
- **In Islam**, marriage (*nikah*) is seen as a sacred contract, a partnership built on love, mercy, and mutual respect: *"And of His signs is that He created for you from yourselves mates that you may find tranquility in them; and He placed between you affection and mercy."* (Qur'an 30:21)
- **In Indigenous Spirituality**, the union between partners is seen as a joining of souls that strengthens not only the individuals but the community as a whole. Ceremonies often honor the sacred commitment to walk life's journey together in harmony.

These teachings remind us that marital love is not merely a personal bond but a sacred act that reflects the unity and interconnectedness of all life.

The Gift of Partnership

The love of a husband or wife is a partnership of equals, each bringing their own strengths, dreams, and vulnerabilities to the relationship. It is a love that grows not despite challenges but because of them, deepening through shared experiences and mutual care.

In marriage, love is not simply given; it is built. It is the daily acts of kindness, the quiet reassurances, the shared laughter, and the steadfast support that create a foundation strong enough to weather life's storms. It is the love that says, *"I see you, I honor you, and I choose you, every day."*

Reflection: The Love That Walks Beside Us

1. *Think of a moment when you felt deeply supported by a partner, whether through words, actions, or simply their presence. How did it strengthen your bond?*
2. *What does your faith or personal philosophy teach about the sacredness of marriage and partnership?*
3. *How can you nurture the love in your relationship, offering patience, understanding, and gratitude for the journey you share?*

Marital Love as a Reflection of One

The love between a husband and wife, or two committed partners, reflects the unity and interconnectedness of life. It is a love that grows through mutual care, sacrifice, and joy, reminding us that true connection is a choice made each day. In its enduring nature, marital love mirrors the infinite: two lives becoming one, and through that union, touching the divine.

Love as the Bridge to One

In every tradition, love is not just a virtue but a force that unites us with the infinite. It is the foundation upon which all faiths are built, the thread that connects us to each other and to One. Love is the bridge that carries us beyond division, beyond ego, into the truth of connection.

Stories of Love Across Faiths

Love transcends time, culture, and belief, weaving itself into the stories that shape and guide humanity. These tales, drawn from the world's faiths, offer glimpses of love's transformative power. They remind us that love is not confined to words or doctrines but is lived and felt in ways that connect us all.

Christianity: The Parable of the Lost Sheep

In Christianity, love is often portrayed as a force that seeks out and saves the lost. The Parable of the Lost Sheep (Luke 15:1–7) tells of a shepherd who leaves ninety-nine sheep to search for the one that has gone astray. When he finds it, he rejoices, carrying the sheep on his shoulders and celebrating its return.

This story is a profound reminder of the value of each individual and the boundless love that refuses to give up on anyone. It teaches that love is not about numbers or convenience—it is about going the extra mile to bring others back to safety and belonging.

Islam: The Woman Who Gave Water to a Dog

In Islam, the value of compassion extends to all beings. The Prophet Muhammad once shared the story of a woman who saw a thirsty dog at a well. Though she had nothing to draw water with, she climbed into the well, filled her shoe with water, and gave it to the dog to drink. Because of her act of mercy, Allah forgave her sins.

This story underscores the idea that love is not limited to humans but encompasses all of creation. It is a call to show kindness to all living things, reflecting the merciful love of Allah.

Hinduism: The Love of Rama and Hanuman

In the Hindu epic *Ramayana*, the bond between Lord Rama and Hanuman exemplifies devotion and selfless love. Hanuman, the devoted servant of Rama, goes to extraordinary lengths to serve him, even leaping across oceans to deliver Rama's message to Sita. When Hanuman is praised for his loyalty, he responds humbly:

- *"I am but your servant, my Lord. My joy comes from serving you."*

This story reflects the idea that love is not about possession but about surrender and devotion. It teaches that true love seeks not personal gain but the joy of uplifting others.

Judaism: Ruth's Love for Naomi

The Book of Ruth in the Hebrew Bible tells the story of Ruth's unwavering loyalty to her mother-in-law, Naomi. After the death of their husbands, Naomi urges Ruth to return to her own people, but Ruth refuses, saying:

- *"Where you go, I will go; where you stay, I will stay. Your people will be my people, and your God my God."* (Ruth 1:16)

Ruth's love for Naomi is a powerful testament to the strength of chosen family. It shows that love is not bound by obligation but is a deliberate choice to stand by someone, even in the face of hardship.

Buddhism: The Bodhisattva's Compassion

In Mahayana Buddhism, the Bodhisattva embodies selfless love and compassion. A Bodhisattva is one who attains enlightenment but chooses to remain in the world to help others achieve liberation.

One story tells of Avalokiteshvara, the Bodhisattva of Compassion, who vowed to save all sentient beings from suffering. Seeing the vastness of their pain, Avalokiteshvara's heart shattered into a thousand pieces. From these fragments, the universe created a thousand arms to help him reach all who were in need.

This story teaches that love is limitless, extending to all beings without discrimination. It reminds us that compassion is an act of strength and that love can heal even the deepest wounds.

Taoism: The Farmer's Son

A Taoist story illustrates the love of acceptance and trust in the natural flow of life. A farmer's son breaks his leg while taming a wild horse. Neighbors pity the boy's misfortune, but the farmer responds, *"Maybe."* Days later, soldiers come to recruit young men for war, but the son is spared because of his injury.

This story reflects the Taoist belief in embracing life's changes with love and equanimity. It teaches that love does not seek to control but trusts the unfolding of the Tao, the natural Way of existence.

Sikhism: Guru Nanak and the Leper

One story from Sikhism tells of Guru Nanak's compassion for a leper shunned by society. When others refused to approach the man, Guru Nanak embraced him, offering both physical and spiritual care.

This act of love demonstrates the Sikh principle of *Ik Onkar*—the belief in the oneness of God and humanity. It reminds us that love sees beyond appearances, embracing all as equals and reflections of the divine.

Shinto: The Sun Goddess Amaterasu

In Shinto mythology, the story of Amaterasu, the Sun Goddess, reflects love as a source of renewal and hope. When Amaterasu retreats into a cave, plunging the world into darkness, the other deities gather to coax her out. They sing, dance, and create laughter, eventually drawing her back into the light.

This story teaches that love is a collective act, one that brings warmth and illumination to the world. It reminds us of the power of community and connection to restore harmony.

Indigenous Spirituality: The Gift of the First Salmon

Among many Indigenous peoples of the Pacific Northwest, the first salmon of the season is honored with a special ceremony. The salmon is seen as a gift from the earth, and its sacrifice ensures the survival of the community.

This tradition reflects a deep love for the natural world and the interconnectedness of all life. It teaches gratitude and reciprocity, reminding us that love is expressed through care for the earth and all its creatures.

Satanism: The Tale of Lilith

In some interpretations of Satanic philosophy, the figure of Lilith—a character from Jewish mythology—is seen as a symbol of independence and self-love. According to legend, Lilith was created as Adam's equal but refused to submit to him. Choosing exile over subjugation, she left the Garden of Eden, embracing her autonomy despite the cost.

This story has been reclaimed by some as a representation of personal empowerment. Lilith's love for herself—her refusal to compromise her dignity—becomes a powerful metaphor for the journey of self-respect and authenticity. It challenges us to consider: What does it mean to love oneself enough to honor one's truth? It means recognizing that within each of us lies a reflection of One—a unique expression of the infinite. To honor your truth is to embrace your connection to the greater whole, stripping away ego and fear to align with the unity that binds us all.

Reflection: What Does Your Faith Teach About Love?

1. *Think of a story from your own faith or tradition that has shaped your understanding of love. How has it influenced your relationships with others?*

2. *How can you embody the love shown in these stories—through acts of compassion, forgiveness, or devotion?*
3. *What would it look like to extend love to someone different from you, recognizing the divine within them?*

These stories from diverse faiths remind us that love is a universal truth, a force that connects us to each other and to the infinite. Each story offers a glimpse of how love can transform, heal, and unite, inviting us to live with greater compassion and connection. Would you like to refine this further or explore additional stories?

Part III: Compassion as the Bridge

Compassion is the practice of love made tangible. It is the hand extended to the weary, the voice that comforts in times of despair, and the quiet act of care that requires nothing in return. Compassion is not confined to any one faith or philosophy; it is the thread that weaves through all traditions, connecting humanity to the divine and to one another. It is through compassion that we bridge the gaps between us, recognizing the shared struggles and joys that make us One.

1. The Power of Compassion

Compassion is transformative. It softens hardened hearts, heals unseen wounds, and creates bonds that transcend differences. Across the world's religions, compassion is celebrated as a sacred act—a way to reflect the divine and nurture unity.

Buddhism: The Practice of Loving-Kindness

In Buddhism, compassion (*karuna*) is not just an ideal but a core practice, cultivated through meditation, mindfulness, and daily action. The Dalai Lama teaches:

- *"If you want others to be happy, practice compassion. If you want to be happy, practice compassion."*

Compassion in Buddhism arises from the recognition of *dukkha* (suffering) as a universal experience. To ease another's suffering is to ease your own, for in the interconnected web of existence, no being is truly separate. The Bodhisattva's vow to remain in the world until all beings are liberated exemplifies this boundless compassion. It is a love that does not rest until every soul is free.

Christianity: Serving the Least Among Us

In Christianity, compassion is seen as a reflection of God's love for humanity. Jesus taught that acts of kindness toward others are acts of kindness toward the divine:

- *"Whatever you did for the least of these, you did for me."* (Matthew 25:40)

This teaching challenges believers to see the face of Christ in the hungry, the sick, the imprisoned, and the forgotten. Compassion is not about grand gestures but about simple acts of care that restore dignity and hope. It reminds us that to serve others is to serve God, and in doing so, we become bridges of love and healing.

Judaism: Saving One Life as Saving the World

The Talmud teaches:

- *"Whoever saves a life, it is as if they have saved the entire world."*

This profound statement reflects Judaism's emphasis on the sanctity of life and the interconnectedness of humanity. Compassion in Judaism is not limited to the immediate act—it ripples outward, touching countless lives. By saving one person, by easing one pain, we honor the divine in all creation.

Compassion in Other Faiths

Compassion is not limited to these traditions; it is a universal principle reflected in countless teachings:

- **Hinduism:** The Mahabharata teaches, *"The wise man does not wish for the happiness of the world by causing pain to other beings."* Compassion is the practice of living in harmony with the world, recognizing the divine in all creatures.
- **Islam:** The Prophet Muhammad said, *"Be merciful to those on earth, and the One above the heavens will have mercy upon you."* Compassion in Islam

is a reflection of Allah's infinite mercy, extended through acts of kindness and justice.

- **Taoism:** Compassion is one of the three treasures of the Tao, alongside humility and simplicity. Laozi writes, *"Compassion leads to courage."* It is through compassion that we align with the natural flow of the universe.

The Symbol of the Bridge

Compassion can be imagined as a bridge—spanning divides, connecting hearts, and uniting paths that might otherwise remain separate. This bridge does not erase differences; it honors them, providing a way for understanding and love to flow freely.

The bridge of compassion is not always easy to cross. It requires courage to step beyond the boundaries of self, to enter the suffering of another with humility and grace. Yet, it is on this bridge that we find the essence of connection, the truth of One.

Reflection: Practicing Compassion

1. *Think of a time when someone showed you compassion. How did it change your perspective or lighten your burden?*
2. *How can you practice compassion today, even in a small way? What barriers might you need to overcome to extend kindness to someone in need?*
3. *What does your faith teach about compassion? How can those teachings guide you in building bridges of understanding and care?*

Compassion as the Heart of One

Compassion is not just a practice; it is a way of being. It is the recognition that we are all connected, that the pain of one is the pain of all, and that the healing of one is the healing of all. In every act of compassion, we step closer to the truth of One, bridging the divides between us with love, humility, and grace.

The Ripple Effect of Compassion

Compassion is not an isolated act; it is a force that flows outward, touching lives in ways we may never fully see or understand. Each act of care creates ripples, spreading far beyond the initial moment, connecting hearts, and inspiring a chain reaction of kindness. Compassion moves through the world like laughter shared in a quiet room or a light kindled in darkness. It is a reminder that through love and understanding, we are part of something far greater than ourselves.

Effect of Compassion

Imagine a single drop of water falling into a still pond. The ripples spread outward in perfect circles, reaching every corner of the surface. Compassion works in much the same way. One act of kindness—a hand extended, a gentle word, a simple gesture of care—creates waves that extend far beyond the moment, touching lives in ways we may never realize.

Consider these ripples:

1. **The Immediate Impact:**
   - The person receiving compassion feels seen, valued, and cared for. In their moment of need, they are reminded of their worth and their connection to others.

2. **The Ripple of Gratitude:**
   - Acts of compassion often inspire gratitude, not just in the recipient but in those who witness it. Gratitude becomes a force of its own, encouraging others to act with kindness.

3. **The Ripple of Inspiration:**
   - Compassion has a way of inspiring others to act. Witnessing or experiencing kindness can prompt someone to offer care in turn, creating a chain of love and connection that expands outward.

Each ripple of compassion carries the essence of One—a truth that connects us all through acts of love and care.

Compassion as a Beacon in Darkness

Compassion has the power to bring light into the darkest places. When someone feels unseen, unheard, or forgotten, an act of compassion becomes a beacon, illuminating their path and reminding them they are not alone. This light grows brighter with each act of care, creating a web of connection that strengthens the entire fabric of humanity.

Even the smallest acts—sharing a meal, listening without judgment, offering a smile—have the power to transform despair into hope. Compassion doesn't just change the moment; it changes the trajectory of lives.

The Courage to Be Compassionate

Compassion is not always easy. It requires us to step outside of ourselves, to see the world through another's eyes, and to offer care without expecting anything in return. It calls for courage—the courage to be vulnerable, to connect, and to act in the face of fear or indifference.

This courage is what makes compassion so powerful. It builds bridges where there were once walls, creating spaces where understanding and love can flourish. Compassion reminds us that even in a divided world, we are capable of connection and unity.

The Multiplier Effect of Love

Compassion doesn't just flow outward; it comes back to us, amplified. When we act with care, we experience the joy of connection and the fulfillment of knowing we have made a difference. This multiplier effect is a reflection of One: the idea that every act of love, no matter how small, contributes to the greater whole.

Think of the moments in your own life when you have received compassion. How did they change you? Did they inspire you to offer the same to others? These moments are not isolated; they are part of a larger movement of love that connects us all.

The Quiet Acts That Change the World

Compassion often works quietly, without fanfare. It is found in the neighbor who checks on an elderly friend, the teacher who stays late to help a struggling student, the stranger who offers a hand to someone who has fallen. These quiet acts may go unnoticed by the world, but their impact is profound.

Each act of compassion is a thread in the tapestry of humanity, weaving together moments of care, kindness, and connection. Over time, these threads create a fabric strong enough to hold us all.

Reflection: The Ripples You Create

1. *Think of a time when someone's compassion changed your life. How did it feel to be on the receiving end of care and understanding?*
2. *What small act of compassion can you offer today, knowing that it might ripple outward in ways you cannot see?*
3. *How does your faith or belief system guide you in practicing compassion, and how can you embody those teachings in your daily life?*

Compassion as a Bridge to One

Compassion is the practice of love in action, a force that connects us to one another and to the infinite. It is the recognition that no one is truly separate, that each life is intertwined with the next. Through compassion, we become the bridge that carries love and understanding into the world, creating ripples that touch the lives of those we may never meet.

In every act of compassion, we move closer to the truth of One—breaking down barriers, healing wounds, and building a world rooted in love and unity.

The Barriers to Compassion

Compassion is one of humanity's greatest gifts, yet it is often the most challenging to practice. Fear, judgment, and division create barriers that keep us from connecting with others in meaningful ways. These barriers are not insurmountable, but they require self-awareness, courage, and the willingness to confront our own limitations. By understanding these obstacles, we can begin to dismantle them, allowing compassion to flow freely.

Fear: The Wall of Self-Protection

Fear is one of the most powerful barriers to compassion. We fear being vulnerable, being hurt, or being rejected. Compassion often requires stepping outside of our comfort zones, and fear can make us hesitant to reach out or engage with others.

For example:

- A person may hesitate to help a stranger in need, fearing rejection or even personal danger.
- Someone might avoid comforting a grieving friend, unsure of what to say or how to act, afraid they might do it "wrong."

Fear is a natural response to uncertainty, but it can isolate us if left unchecked. To overcome fear, we must cultivate courage—the courage to act even when we are unsure, trusting that our intentions matter more than perfection.

Judgment: The Illusion of Superiority

Judgment creates separation where there should be connection. When we judge others—whether for their choices, their circumstances, or their differences—we dehumanize them, making it easier to withhold compassion. Judgment often stems from our own insecurities or misunderstandings, projecting onto others what we fear or dislike in ourselves.

For example:

- A wealthy person may judge someone experiencing homelessness as "lazy" or "undeserving," failing to see the complex circumstances that led to their situation.
- A parent might judge another for parenting differently, rather than recognizing the shared challenges of raising children.

Judgment blocks compassion by creating an "us vs. them" mindset. To overcome judgment, we must practice humility, acknowledging that we do not know the full story of another's life. Compassion grows when we replace judgment with curiosity and empathy.

Division: The Illusion of Separation

Division, whether based on race, religion, politics, or socioeconomic status, is one of the greatest barriers to compassion. When we see others as fundamentally different from ourselves, it becomes harder to extend care and understanding.

For example:

- Cultural or religious differences may lead to misunderstandings or mistrust, preventing acts of kindness or collaboration.
- Political polarization can make people view one another as enemies, forgetting their shared humanity.

Division thrives on the illusion that we are separate, that our differences outweigh our commonalities. To overcome division, we must seek connection—looking for the shared experiences, hopes, and fears that bind us together as One.

Forgiveness: A Radical Act of Compassion

Forgiveness is one of the most profound and radical acts of compassion. It requires letting go of resentment, anger, and the desire for retribution. Forgiveness is not about condoning harm but about freeing ourselves and others from the chains of past pain.

For example:

- In Christianity, Jesus' words on the cross, *"Father, forgive them, for they know not what they do,"* (Luke 23:34) embody the ultimate act of forgiveness, offering grace even in the face of immense suffering.
- In Buddhism, the practice of forgiveness is seen as a way to release anger and cultivate peace. The Buddha taught that holding onto anger is like holding a hot coal, intending to throw it at someone else, but burning yourself instead.
- In Indigenous traditions, forgiveness is often woven into reconciliation ceremonies, allowing communities to heal from generational wounds.

Forgiveness dismantles the barriers of fear, judgment, and division. It is a courageous act that transforms pain into understanding, offering a pathway to connection and healing.

How Compassion Breaks Down Barriers

Compassion is not about erasing differences or ignoring wrongs; it is about choosing connection over separation. When we practice compassion, we create a space where fear, judgment, and division no longer hold power.

1. **Compassion Overcomes Fear:**
    - Compassion requires us to step outside of ourselves, offering care even when it feels uncomfortable or uncertain. Each act of compassion strengthens our courage, proving that love is greater than fear.

2. **Compassion Replaces Judgment:**
   - When we choose compassion, we see others not as "other" but as reflections of ourselves. Judgment fades when we recognize that every person carries their own struggles and stories.
3. **Compassion Heals Division:**
   - Compassion reminds us that our shared humanity is greater than our differences. It builds bridges where walls once stood, creating spaces for understanding and unity.

Reflection: Dismantling Your Barriers

1. *What fears keep you from acting with compassion? How can you begin to confront those fears, even in small ways?*
2. *Think of a time when you judged someone unfairly. How might compassion have changed the way you saw or treated them?*
3. *What divisions in your life could be healed through acts of compassion, forgiveness, or understanding?*

Compassion as the Great Equalizer

The barriers to compassion—fear, judgment, and division—are not permanent. They are illusions created by the ego, designed to keep us separate. Compassion dissolves these illusions, reminding us that we are all connected, all part of the same infinite whole. Each act of compassion is a step closer to the truth of One, a reminder that love, understanding, and care are bridges strong enough to overcome any obstacle.

Acting with Compassion

Compassion is not reserved for grand gestures or extraordinary circumstances; it is found in the quiet, daily acts that weave love and care into the fabric of life. These moments of kindness, often unnoticed by the world, have the power to transform not only the recipient but also the giver.

Compassion in action is how we embody the truth of One, bridging the gaps between us and nurturing the connections that sustain humanity.

Small Acts, Profound Impact

Compassion is a practice, not a performance. It is cultivated in the seemingly simple ways we choose to care for others, making small ripples that create a larger wave of love and unity. These acts may appear minor, but their impact is profound.

1. **A Kind Word:**

A simple compliment, a word of encouragement, or a heartfelt thank-you can lift someone's spirit, reminding them that they are valued and seen.

Example: Complimenting a colleague on their hard work or thanking a barista for their kindness can brighten their day in ways we might never know.

2. **A Listening Ear:**

Offering someone your full attention is one of the most powerful acts of compassion. To truly listen is to say, *"You matter. Your story matters."*

Example: Listening to a friend without interrupting or offering solutions creates a space for them to feel heard and understood.

3. **Helping a Stranger:**

Small acts of service—a helping hand, holding a door open, or offering directions—can create moments of connection, even with those we may never see again.

Example: Helping someone carry heavy bags or paying for a stranger's coffee reminds us of our shared humanity.

These small acts are not insignificant. They are threads in the tapestry of connection, each one strengthening the bonds that tie us to each other and to the infinite.

The Courage of Everyday Compassion

Acting with compassion often requires courage. It asks us to look beyond our own needs and step into the world of another. It calls us to be present, to offer care without expectation, and to recognize that even the smallest gestures can carry profound meaning.

Consider the courage it takes to:

- Approach someone who looks lonely and offer a smile or a conversation.
- Extend forgiveness to someone who has hurt you, creating space for healing.
- Advocate for someone who cannot advocate for themselves, using your voice to amplify theirs.

These acts may seem small in scale, but they are immense in their impact. Compassion creates a ripple effect, spreading far beyond the moment, touching lives in ways we may never see.

Compassion in the Mundane

Compassion does not always require us to go out of our way. It can be integrated into the ordinary rhythms of life:

- **In the Workplace:** Offering to help a colleague meet a deadline or simply asking, *"How are you, really?"*
- **In the Community:** Checking in on an elderly neighbor or volunteering at a local food bank.
- **At Home:** Showing patience with a child, a partner, or a sibling when tensions rise.

Each of these moments, though small, carries the weight of love and care. They remind us that compassion is not about changing the world all at once but about changing the moment for someone else.

The Gift of Presence

Compassion is often as simple as showing up fully for someone else. In a world filled with distractions, being present is one of the greatest gifts we can give.

- Sitting with a friend who is grieving, even in silence, speaks volumes.
- Taking time to truly connect with a family member reminds them they are not alone.

These acts of presence are profound because they create spaces of safety, love, and connection—spaces where healing and unity can flourish.

Reflection: Compassion in Action

1. *Think of a time when someone showed you compassion through a small gesture. How did it make you feel? What impact did it have on your day or your outlook?*
2. *What small act of compassion can you offer today? How might it create ripples of kindness and connection?*
3. *How does your faith or belief system inspire you to act with compassion, even in the smallest ways?*

Compassion as a Daily Practice

Compassion is not about perfection; it is about presence. It is the daily choice to act with love, to care for those around us, and to build bridges of understanding and connection. In each small act of kindness, we reflect the truth of One: that we are not separate, that we are all part of something greater, and that our actions, no matter how small, carry infinite meaning.

Part IV: Unity in Diversity

Unity is not the erasure of differences but the harmony that arises when we embrace them. Each person, culture, and faith offers a unique perspective on the divine, contributing to the greater whole. Unity in diversity reflects the truth of One: that while we may walk different paths, we are all connected, sharing the same essence and purpose.

The world's religions celebrate this unity, not by demanding uniformity but by honoring the infinite ways humanity connects to the divine. Each tradition teaches that diversity is not a barrier but a gift—a way to see the infinite reflected in countless forms.

1. The Beauty of Many Paths

Across faiths, unity is celebrated as a truth that transcends divisions. Each tradition emphasizes that while practices, rituals, and beliefs may differ, the ultimate goal is the same: connection with the divine and with one another.

Hinduism: Seeing the Divine in All Beings

Hinduism offers a profound vision of unity through the concept of *Brahman*, the ultimate reality that underlies all existence. The Upanishads teach:

- *"He who sees all beings in himself and himself in all beings, attains the highest."*

This verse reflects the Hindu understanding that the divine essence (*Atman*) within each individual is not separate from the universal reality (*Brahman*). To recognize this unity is to move beyond the illusion of separateness (*maya*), seeing all beings as interconnected.

Hindu stories often illustrate this truth. In the *Bhagavad Gita*, Lord Krishna reveals his divine form to Arjuna, showing that all creation is part of the same infinite reality. This moment reminds us that diversity is not a contradiction but an expression of unity, a reflection of the divine in countless forms.

Islam: Brotherhood and Equality

In Islam, unity is expressed through the principle of *Ummah*, the global community of believers united in submission to Allah. The Qur'an declares:

- *"The believers are but a single brotherhood."* (Qur'an 49:10)

This verse underscores the idea that humanity, regardless of race, nationality, or language, is one family under Allah. During the *hajj* pilgrimage, millions of Muslims from every corner of the world gather at Mecca, dressed in simple white garments, erasing distinctions of wealth, status, or ethnicity. This powerful act of unity demonstrates that diversity within the *Ummah* strengthens rather than divides it.

Islam also teaches respect for other faiths, recognizing that all prophets—from Adam to Muhammad—were sent by the same God. This acknowledgment of shared spiritual heritage reinforces the idea that unity exists even among diverse religious traditions.

Judaism: The Oneness of God and Creation

In Judaism, unity is central to the Shema prayer, a daily declaration of faith:

- *"Hear, O Israel: The Lord our God, the Lord is one."* (Deuteronomy 6:4)

This affirmation of God's oneness is not merely theological; it is a call to action. To recognize God's unity is to recognize the interconnectedness of all creation. It reminds believers that there is no division between the sacred and the ordinary, between God and humanity.

The prophetic tradition in Judaism emphasizes justice and compassion as expressions of unity. The Talmud teaches that saving a single life is equivalent to saving an entire world, reflecting the intrinsic value and interconnectedness of every individual.

Christianity: One Body in Christ

Christianity speaks of unity through the metaphor of the body of Christ. The Apostle Paul writes:

- *"Just as a body, though one, has many parts, but all its many parts form one body, so it is with Christ."* (1 Corinthians 12:12)

This imagery illustrates that each person, with their unique gifts and roles, contributes to the greater whole. Diversity is not a weakness but a strength, enriching the community and reflecting the fullness of divine love.

The story of Pentecost further highlights unity in diversity. When the Holy Spirit descends upon the disciples, they begin speaking in different languages, allowing people from many nations to hear the message of God in their own tongues. This moment symbolizes the universality of God's love, reaching all people regardless of their differences.

Buddhism: The Interconnected Web of Existence

Buddhism teaches unity through the principle of *pratityasamutpada* (dependent origination), which reveals that all phenomena arise in dependence upon other phenomena. This interconnectedness means that no being exists in isolation; all are part of a vast web of existence.

The metaphor of Indra's Net captures this beautifully: an infinite web stretches across the cosmos, with a jewel at each intersection. Each jewel reflects every other jewel, illustrating the unity and interdependence of all beings.

Buddhism's emphasis on compassion arises from this understanding. To care for another is to care for oneself, as all life is interconnected.

Sikhism: The Unity of God and Humanity

Sikhism emphasizes *Ik Onkar*, the oneness of God, as its central teaching. This belief extends to humanity, affirming that all people are equal regardless of caste, gender, or religion. Guru Nanak declared:

- *"There is no Hindu, there is no Muslim."*

This statement reflects Sikhism's rejection of divisions and its embrace of unity. In Sikh practice, the community kitchen (*langar*) embodies this principle, serving meals to all, side by side, without distinction. Through such acts, Sikhs demonstrate that unity is not theoretical but lived.

Taoism: Harmony in Balance

In Taoism, unity is found in the balance of opposites, symbolized by the *yin-yang*. This iconic image represents the interplay of complementary forces—light and dark, active and passive, masculine and feminine. Together, these forces create harmony, reflecting the Tao, the ultimate principle that connects all things.

Laozi writes:

- *"The Tao is great. All things depend on it for life, and it does not turn away from them."*

This teaching reminds us that diversity is not a source of conflict but a necessary element of harmony. Each aspect of existence, no matter how different, contributes to the greater whole.

Shinto: Unity Through Nature and Ritual

Shinto honors the *kami*, spiritual presences that inhabit all aspects of the natural world. Each mountain, river, tree, and creature carries its own unique spirit, yet all are connected within the sacred flow of life.

The *matsuri* festivals in Shinto celebrate this unity, bringing communities together to honor the *kami* and the cycles of nature. These rituals remind participants that they are part of something larger, connected to the earth, the divine, and each other.

Satanism: Embracing Individuality Within the Whole

In Modern Satanism, unity is found not in conformity but in the celebration of individuality. While often misunderstood, Satanism's teachings emphasize personal empowerment, ethical boundaries, and authenticity, reflecting a unique perspective on unity in diversity.

Anton LaVey writes: *"Man is his own god."* This philosophy invites individuals to embrace their unique essence while recognizing their role within the greater whole. Satanism teaches that by honoring one's individuality, one contributes to the collective harmony. It reminds us that diversity strengthens connection when rooted in mutual respect and understanding.

The principles of Modern Satanism, such as respecting boundaries and acting with authenticity, challenge the notion that unity requires uniformity. Instead, they highlight that true unity arises when differences are honored, and individuality is celebrated as part of the infinite mosaic of existence.

Satanism, with its emphasis on self-awareness and ethical authenticity, reminds us that unity does not erase difference but celebrates it. By challenging us to think critically and respect individuality, it contributes to the universal truth of One: that every unique voice and perspective is part of the infinite whole.

Reflection: Embracing Unity in Diversity

1. *Think of a time when you encountered someone whose beliefs or background differed from yours. How did you find common ground?*
2. *What does your faith teach about unity? How can those teachings guide you to see diversity as a source of strength and connection?*
3. *How can you celebrate the differences in your community while recognizing the shared humanity that unites us all?*

Unity in Diversity as a Reflection of One

The beauty of many paths lies not in their sameness but in their shared destination. Each tradition, with its unique perspective, contributes to the greater truth of One: that we are all connected, all part of the same infinite whole. By embracing unity in diversity, we honor the richness of humanity and the divine love that binds us together.

The Symbolism of Unity

The image of three hands converging at a single point is a profound reminder of unity across all dimensions—time, space, and belief. These hands, rising together, symbolize the coming together of what may seem separate: past, present, and future; mind, body, and spirit; you, me, and the divine. Past mind you, Present body me, Future spirit One. At their point of convergence, all division dissolves, and what remains is a brilliant unity—a reminder that we are not and have never been truly separate.

Unity Across Time

The convergence of past, present, and future reflects the timeless nature of connection. Each moment carries echoes of what came before and seeds of what is yet to come. Compassion, love, and understanding transcend time, weaving threads that bind us to one another across generations.

In faith traditions, time itself is often seen as cyclical or eternal, emphasizing the interconnectedness of all that has been, is, and will be:

- In **Hinduism**, the cycles of creation, preservation, and transformation reflect the ongoing unity of existence.
- In **Christianity**, the eternal nature of God's love connects past covenants with present faith and future hope.
- In **Indigenous Spirituality**, the stories of ancestors live on, guiding the present and shaping the future.

Unity across time reminds us that our actions today ripple forward, carrying love, understanding, and connection into the future.

Unity Across Space

The three hands also symbolize unity across space, breaking down the illusion of separation created by borders, cultures, and traditions. Though we may speak different languages, follow different paths, and live in distant lands, the same truth flows through us all. The space between us is not empty—it is filled with the energy of connection, the invisible threads of One.

Consider how faiths reflect this unity:

- In **Islam**, the global *Ummah* reminds believers that they are part of a single brotherhood, transcending nationality and ethnicity.
- In **Sikhism**, the practice of *langar*—a shared meal open to all—embodies the idea that no matter where we come from, we are equals.
- In **Shinto**, the reverence for nature's *kami* illustrates the shared sacredness of the earth, connecting all who walk upon it.

Unity across space calls us to see the divine not as confined to one place or people but present everywhere, connecting us in ways that transcend physical distance.

Unity Across Beliefs

The convergence of the hands also represents the unity of diverse beliefs, traditions, and perspectives. Though each hand may represent a different path, they rise together toward the same truth. This reminds us that the essence of One is not about erasing differences but about embracing them as expressions of the infinite.

- **In Judaism**, the Shema prayer declares the oneness of God, calling believers to live in harmony with creation.
- **In Buddhism**, the understanding of interconnectedness teaches that all beings are part of the same web of existence.
- **In Taoism**, the balance of yin and yang reflects the harmony that arises from diversity.

Unity across beliefs invites us to see the divine reflected in every path, recognizing that each perspective contributes to the greater whole.

The Hands as a Reflection of One

The image of the hands converging speaks not only of unity but also of action. These hands do not remain idle; they rise, reaching toward something greater. They remind us that unity is not passive—it requires us to extend our hands to one another, to build bridges, and to act with love and understanding.

When we reach out, we affirm the truth of One: that we are stronger together, that our differences are not barriers but gifts, and that connection is the foundation of all existence.

Reflection: Bridging Differences

1. *Think of someone whose beliefs or experiences differ from yours. What can you learn from their perspective? How might their story expand your understanding of connection?*
2. *In what ways can you extend your hand—metaphorically or literally—to someone who may feel distant from you?*
3. *How does recognizing unity across time, space, and belief change the way you approach your relationships and your world?*

Unity as the Essence of One

The image of hands converging at a single point reminds us that unity is not about sameness—it is about connection. It is the coming together of all that we are—our past, present, and future; our mind, body, and spirit; our individual paths and our shared truths. This convergence is where the light shines brightest, where division gives way to love, and where the infinite truth of One becomes undeniable.

The Universal Symbols of Unity

Symbols have the power to transcend words, cultures, and traditions, offering a shared language for expressing profound truths. Across the world's religions and philosophies, certain symbols emerge repeatedly, speaking to the universal understanding of unity. These symbols remind us that beneath our differences lies a shared essence, a connection that binds all existence together. Among the most enduring symbols of unity are the Ouroboros, Mandalas, and the Tree of Life, each carrying a unique yet universal message of interconnectedness, eternity, and the infinite.

The Ouroboros: Unity Through Eternity

The Ouroboros, a serpent or dragon devouring its own tail, is one of the oldest symbols of eternity and unity. Originating in ancient Egypt and later adopted by Greek, Norse, and alchemical traditions, the Ouroboros represents the cyclical nature of existence—the eternal return of life, death, and rebirth.

- **In Egyptian Mythology:** The Ouroboros was linked to the sun's daily journey, symbolizing renewal and the eternal cycle of creation.
- **In Alchemy:** It represents the unity of opposites, the merging of beginning and end, and the interconnectedness of all things.

The Ouroboros reminds us that life is not linear but cyclical, that every ending is a new beginning. It speaks to the truth that all things are connected in an unbroken circle, reflecting the infinite essence of One.

Mandalas: Cosmic Unity

Mandalas, intricate geometric patterns found in Hinduism, Buddhism, and Indigenous traditions, are profound symbols of cosmic unity. These sacred designs represent the universe itself, with each layer drawing the viewer inward toward the center, a point of ultimate stillness and connection.

- **In Hinduism and Buddhism:** Mandalas are used in meditation to symbolize the journey toward enlightenment. Each element of the mandala reflects aspects of existence, showing how all things are interwoven.
- **In Indigenous Traditions:** Circular designs in art and rituals symbolize the cycle of life, the seasons, and the unity of nature and spirit.

The mandala invites us to see the divine pattern within ourselves and the world. Its symmetry reflects the balance of existence, and its center reminds us of the One at the heart of all things.

The Tree of Life: Interconnection and Growth

The Tree of Life appears in countless cultures and religions, symbolizing the interconnectedness of all existence. Its roots dig deep into the earth, its branches stretch toward the heavens, and its trunk unites the two, embodying the balance between the physical and spiritual realms.

- **In Christianity:** The Tree of Life in the Garden of Eden represents eternal life and divine connection.
- **In Norse Mythology:** Yggdrasil, the World Tree, connects the nine realms of existence, sustaining the universe with its strength.
- **In Kabbalah:** The Tree of Life is a mystical diagram of the *sefirot*, emanations of divine energy that sustain creation.
- **In Indigenous Spirituality:** Trees symbolize wisdom, community, and the cyclical nature of life. For example, the Haudenosaunee (Iroquois) revere the Tree of Peace, under which warring nations buried their weapons to form unity.

The Tree of Life teaches us that while we may grow in different directions, we are all rooted in the same earth and nourished by the same source. It is a living metaphor for Ɵne, showing that diversity and unity coexist in harmony.

The Baphomet (Modern Satanism): Unity in Individuality and Duality

The very act of embracing a religion like Modern Satanism reflects a unity in individuality—a celebration of personal empowerment and the courage to walk one's own path. The Baphomet, a central symbol in Satanism, embodies this unity through duality. Depicted with human and animal features, masculine and feminine qualities, and celestial and earthly elements, the Baphomet represents the interconnectedness of opposites.

Its message is clear: light and dark, mind and body, good and evil are not adversaries but complementary aspects of the whole. Like the Taoist *yin-yang*, the Baphomet teaches that balance and contrast are essential to understanding the infinite. Its provocative imagery challenges conventional norms, encouraging critical thought and intellectual rebellion—not to create division, but to foster deeper understanding and connection.

At its core, the Baphomet reflects the universal truth of One: that unity arises not from erasing differences but from embracing complexity and celebrating the harmony of opposites.

Other Universal Symbols of Unity

1. The Yin-Yang (Taoism):

The Taoist symbol of balance and harmony illustrates the interconnectedness of opposites. Light and dark, active and passive, masculine and feminine—each is incomplete without the other. Together, they create a unified whole, reflecting the Tao, the ultimate principle of existence.

2. The Flame (Zoroastrianism, Hinduism, and Buddhism):

A flame represents both individuality and unity. While each flame is unique, all fire shares the same essence. It illuminates the path, warms the spirit, and connects us to the divine truth of eternity.

3. The Circle (Indigenous Traditions):

In many Indigenous cultures, the circle represents the cycles of life, the unity of community, and the connection between earth and spirit. Ceremonial dances, storytelling circles, and art reflect this sacred shape, emphasizing that everything is connected.

Reflection: Finding Symbols in Your Own Life

1. *What symbols in your faith or culture speak to unity and connection? How do they inspire you to see the infinite in the everyday?*
2. *How can symbols like the Ouroboros, mandalas, or the Tree of Life deepen your understanding of interconnectedness?*

3. *What would it mean to see these symbols not just as representations but as invitations to live with love, balance, and unity?*

Symbols as Pathways to One

The Ouroboros, mandalas, the Tree of Life and the Baphomet are not just images; they are mirrors reflecting the universal truth of One. They teach us that unity does not erase individuality but celebrates it as part of a greater whole. These symbols invite us to look beyond the surface, to see the sacred patterns that connect us, and to remember that we are all part of the same infinite design.

Moments of Connection

Moments of connection are profound and transformative. They are the instances when we feel a part of something greater than ourselves—when the barriers of ego dissolve, and we glimpse the infinite unity that binds us all. These experiences are not confined to one culture, faith, or context; they are universal, arising in the sacred and the ordinary alike. By reflecting on these moments, we uncover the threads that connect us to the divine, to one another, and to the truth of One.

The Universality of Connection

Across faiths and traditions, moments of connection are seen as glimpses of the divine:

- **In Christianity,** such moments may occur during prayer or worship, when believers feel God's presence surrounding and uplifting them.
- **In Buddhism,** connection is found in the quiet of meditation, when the practitioner transcends the self and experiences unity with all beings.
- **In Indigenous Spirituality,** connection often comes through rituals that honor the earth, reminding participants of their place within the web of life.

- **In Islam**, moments of connection arise in submission to Allah, as in the act of prostration during prayer, which symbolizes humility and unity with the Creator.

These moments are universal reminders that while our paths may differ, the connection we seek is the same.

Moments in the Sacred and the Everyday

Moments of connection are not always grand or extraordinary. Often, they arise in the quiet, the simple, and the unnoticed:

- Watching the sun rise, feeling the warmth of its light on your skin, and sensing the rhythm of the universe.
- Standing in a forest, hearing the rustle of leaves and the distant call of birds, feeling deeply connected to the earth.
- Holding the hand of a loved one, feeling the unspoken bond that transcends words.
- Sharing a meal with others, recognizing the act of nourishment as both physical and spiritual.

These moments remind us that connection is always present, waiting to be noticed.

The Power of Shared Connection

Connection is amplified when shared. It is found in the laughter of friends, the unity of a crowd singing together, or the collective silence of a prayer circle. These shared moments dissolve the illusion of separateness, reminding us that we are stronger together.

- **In Sikhism**, the practice of *langar*—sharing a meal with the community—symbolizes unity and equality.
- **In Taoism**, harmony is found in the balance of relationships, where connection strengthens the flow of the Tao.

- **In Judaism**, the communal observance of the Sabbath brings families and communities together, reflecting the sanctity of connection.

These shared experiences invite us to see the divine in one another, deepening our sense of unity.

Moments of Challenge and Connection

Moments of connection often arise not just in joy but also in challenge. They come when we comfort someone in pain, offer forgiveness, or stand together in adversity.

- In these moments, compassion bridges divides, and we find ourselves united by shared humanity.
- These experiences remind us that connection is not just about similarity but about the courage to reach across differences and extend love.

Reflection: Finding Your Moments of Connection

1. *Think of a time when you felt deeply connected to something larger than yourself—whether through nature, community, or a moment of stillness. What did it reveal to you about your place in the world?*
2. *How can you cultivate moments of connection in your daily life? What small practices or rituals might open you to a greater sense of unity?*
3. *What does your faith or philosophy teach about connection, and how can those teachings guide you in building bridges of understanding and love?*

Connection as a Reflection of One

Moments of connection remind us that we are never truly alone. They reveal the threads that bind us to one another, to the earth, and to the infinite. By reflecting on these moments, we see the truth of One—not as an abstract idea but as a lived experience, present in every breath, every relationship, and every act of care.

Part V: Purpose as a Sacred Gift

Purpose is not just a goal or a task; it is the way we live out love, compassion, and unity in the world. Across faiths and traditions, purpose is seen as a sacred calling—a way to align with the divine and contribute to the greater whole. It is through purpose that we give meaning to our lives, honor the sacred, and reflect the truth of One.

Purpose varies across cultures and individuals, yet at its heart, it carries a universal essence: to live with intention, to care for others, and to leave the world brighter than we found it.

1. Finding Purpose Across Faiths

Each religion offers unique insights into purpose, guiding followers to discover their role in the divine plan and the greater web of existence.

Christianity: Created for Good Works

In Christianity, purpose is deeply rooted in the belief that humanity is created in the image of God, called to reflect divine love through action. The Apostle Paul writes:

- *"For we are God's handiwork, created in Christ Jesus to do good works, which God prepared in advance for us to do."* (Ephesians 2:10)

This verse emphasizes that purpose is not just about personal fulfillment but about serving others. Christians are called to be the hands and feet of Christ, living out their faith through acts of kindness, justice, and compassion.

The life of Jesus serves as the ultimate example of purpose fulfilled: healing the sick, feeding the hungry, and loving the marginalized. Through these actions, believers are reminded that purpose is a sacred gift, a way to reflect God's love in the world.

Islam: Worship as Life's Purpose

In Islam, purpose is expressed as submission to Allah's will, recognizing that every aspect of life is an opportunity to worship. The Qur'an declares:

- *"And I did not create mankind except to worship Me."* (Qur'an 51:56)

Worship in Islam is not confined to prayer or rituals; it encompasses all actions performed with intention and sincerity. Caring for one's family, seeking knowledge, and serving the community are all acts of worship when done in alignment with Allah's guidance.

The concept of *niyyah* (intention) highlights the importance of purpose in every action, reminding Muslims that even the smallest deeds can carry profound spiritual significance when rooted in love and devotion.

Buddhism: Walking the Eightfold Path

In Buddhism, purpose is found in the pursuit of enlightenment, guided by the Eightfold Path:

1. Right View
2. Right Intention
3. Right Speech
4. Right Action
5. Right Livelihood
6. Right Effort
7. Right Mindfulness
8. Right Concentration

This path is not a rigid doctrine but a practical guide for living with wisdom, compassion, and balance. It teaches that purpose is not about achieving external success but about cultivating inner peace and contributing to the well-being of others.

Through meditation, ethical living, and mindful action, Buddhists discover purpose as a way to align their lives with the interconnected web of existence.

Hinduism: Fulfilling Dharma

In Hinduism, purpose is deeply tied to *dharma*—the sacred duty that aligns individuals with the cosmic order. The Bhagavad Gita teaches:

- *"Better to do one's own duty imperfectly than to do another's duty perfectly."* (Bhagavad Gita 3:35)

This verse emphasizes that purpose is unique to each person, shaped by their roles, talents, and circumstances. Whether as a parent, teacher, or artist, fulfilling one's *dharma* is seen as a way to honor the divine and contribute to the greater good.

Hinduism reminds us that purpose is not about comparison or competition but about authenticity and devotion, living in harmony with oneself and the universe.

Judaism: Repairing the World (Tikkun Olam)

In Judaism, purpose is expressed through *tikkun olam*, the idea of repairing the world. This concept calls believers to act with justice, kindness, and humility, reflecting God's love through their actions.

The prophet Micah captures this purpose beautifully:

- *"What does the Lord require of you? To act justly, to love mercy, and to walk humbly with your God."* (Micah 6:8)

For Jews, purpose is not abstract but practical, lived out through mitzvot (commandments) and acts of service. It is a way to bring holiness into the everyday, transforming the world one action at a time.

Sikhism: Living in Service

In Sikhism, purpose is centered on *seva* (selfless service) and living in alignment with *Ik Onkar* (the oneness of God). Guru Nanak taught:

- "The best way to find yourself is to lose yourself in the service of others."

Sikhs believe that purpose is not about seeking personal gain but about uplifting others, creating harmony, and reflecting divine love through action. The community kitchen (*langar*) exemplifies this purpose, offering free meals to all as a demonstration of equality and compassion.

Taoism: Flowing with the Tao

In Taoism, purpose is not something to be forced or achieved but something to be discovered by aligning with the Tao—the natural flow of existence. Laozi writes:

- "The Tao does nothing, yet nothing is left undone."

This teaching reminds us that purpose is found in living authentically, in harmony with the rhythms of nature and life. Taoism invites us to let go of resistance and trust the unfolding of the Tao, allowing purpose to emerge naturally.

Shinto: Honoring the Kami

In Shinto, purpose is expressed through gratitude, reverence, and harmony with the *kami*—the spiritual presences that inhabit all things. Shinto teaches that purpose is not about achieving greatness but about honoring the sacredness of the everyday.

Through rituals, offerings, and festivals, followers of Shinto express their purpose by living in balance with nature and celebrating life's blessings. This practice reminds us that purpose can be found in the smallest acts of care and connection.

Indigenous Spirituality: Living in Reciprocity

In Indigenous Spirituality, purpose is deeply tied to the principles of reciprocity and respect for all relations. The Lakota teaching of *Mitákuye Oyás'iŋ* ("All My Relations") reflects the understanding that humanity is part of a larger web of life, with a responsibility to care for the earth and its inhabitants.

Purpose is found in acts that honor this interconnectedness, whether through storytelling, stewardship of the land, or community ceremonies. It is a way of living that nurtures balance and ensures the well-being of future generations.

Satanism: Authenticity and Individual Empowerment

In Modern Satanism, purpose is centered on authenticity and the empowerment of the individual. Anton LaVey writes:

"Life is the great indulgence—death, the great abstinence. Therefore, make the most of life—HERE AND NOW!"

Satanism teaches that purpose is not prescribed by external forces but discovered through self-awareness, critical thought, and the courage to live authentically. It challenges followers to take responsibility for their lives, embracing their individuality while respecting the boundaries of others.

Reflection: Discovering Your Purpose

1. *What does your faith or philosophy teach about purpose? How do these teachings guide your daily actions and decisions?*
2. *How can living with intention help you align with love, compassion, and unity?*
3. *What small steps can you take today to fulfill your unique role in the greater whole?*

Purpose as a Reflection of One

Purpose is not about achieving perfection but about living with intention. It is the way we express love, compassion, and unity in the world, each in our own unique way. Across all faiths, purpose is seen as a sacred gift—a way to connect with the divine, serve others, and reflect the infinite truth of One.

Living with Intention

Living with intention means aligning our actions with our values and purpose, creating a life that reflects love, compassion, and unity. It is not about perfection or grand gestures but about the conscious choice to live meaningfully in each moment. Across faiths and traditions, living with intention is seen as a way to bring the sacred into the everyday—a practice of turning ordinary acts into reflections of divine purpose.

When we live with intention, we recognize that our lives are interconnected with the lives of others and with the greater whole. It is through this recognition that we find purpose in serving others, nurturing relationships, and honoring the divine in all we do.

Serving Others: Purpose Through Compassion

One of the clearest expressions of living with intention is serving others. Acts of service, whether small or large, reflect our shared humanity and the sacred connection we have with one another.

- **In Christianity**, Jesus modeled a life of service, washing the feet of his disciples and teaching that *"the greatest among you will be your servant."* (Matthew 23:11) This act of humility reminds us that service is not about hierarchy but about love and care.
- **In Sikhism**, the practice of *seva* (selfless service) is a central tenet, demonstrated through the community kitchen (*langar*), which serves meals to all regardless of status or faith.

- **In Islam,** service is a form of worship, as seen in the concept of *sadaqah* (charitable giving), which emphasizes helping those in need with intention and sincerity.

Serving others does not require extraordinary circumstances. It can be as simple as helping a neighbor, volunteering at a local shelter, or offering a listening ear. Each act of service, no matter how small, becomes a thread in the fabric of unity.

Finding Joy in Work: Purpose Through Contribution and Passion

Work is often seen as a necessity—a means to survive, to earn, to fulfill obligations. But what if work could be more than that? What if it could be an expression of joy, passion, and purpose? Across faiths and philosophies, there is a recognition that when work is approached with intention and love, it ceases to be a burden and becomes a sacred act—a way to align with the divine, contribute to the greater whole, and reflect the truth of One.

Work, in its truest sense, is not defined by monetary value or external recognition. It is the act of bringing our unique gifts into the world, creating something meaningful, and finding fulfillment in the process. When we find joy in what we do, the lines between work and life blur, and every task becomes an offering—a reflection of love, passion, and unity.

Work as Sacred Action

In many traditions, work is seen not as a chore but as a spiritual practice—a way to honor the divine and contribute to the world:

- **In Hinduism,** the concept of *karma yoga* teaches that work done with selflessness and devotion becomes a path to spiritual growth. The Bhagavad Gita encourages: *"Perform your duty without attachment, and you will attain the supreme."* This teaching reminds us that work, when approached with love and detachment from outcomes, becomes an act of worship.

- **In Judaism,** work is a way to participate in *tikkun olam* (repairing the world). It is seen as a partnership with God, a way to bring holiness into the everyday through acts of creativity, care, and contribution.
- **In Taoism,** work aligned with the Tao becomes effortless and harmonious. Laozi writes: *"The Tao does nothing, yet nothing is left undone."* This teaching invites us to flow with the natural rhythms of life, finding joy and balance in our efforts.

These teachings remind us that work, when infused with intention, can transcend its mundane nature and become a reflection of purpose and connection.

Finding Joy in What We Do

The key to transforming work into joy lies not in changing what we do but in changing how we approach it. When we align our actions with our values, find meaning in our contributions, and embrace the present moment, work becomes a source of fulfillment rather than a means to an end.

Imagine an artist lost in the act of creation, a teacher inspired by their students' growth, or a caretaker offering comfort to someone in need. In these moments, the concept of "work" dissolves, replaced by passion, love, and purpose. But what if that is not your reality? What if the tasks before you feel heavy, disconnected from your essence, and devoid of joy?

To live with true purpose, we must find the place where our soul aligns with our actions—a space where joy flows naturally, and work becomes an expression of love and connection. If you find yourself far from that place, it is not a failure but an invitation. It is a call to reflect, to realign, and to rediscover your unique path to joy.

The Importance of Finding Your Own True Joy

Not all work will resonate with our innermost passions. Sometimes, we find ourselves in roles or environments that feel at odds with our true selves. These moments can feel like disconnects, but they are also opportunities to ask important questions:

- *What brings me true joy?*
- *What lights my spirit and makes me feel alive?*
- *How can I bring more of myself into what I do?*

True joy is not a luxury—it is a reflection of our connection to the infinite. It is the state of being fully alive, fully present, and fully aligned with our values and passions. When we find that joy, we cease to feel constrained by the labels of "work" or "duty." Instead, life becomes a flow of creativity, purpose, and love.

When Joy Feels Far Away

If you are not where you truly feel you should be, it is essential to honor that awareness. Recognizing disconnection is the first step toward rediscovering joy.

- **In Christianity,** the story of the Prodigal Son reminds us that even when we stray far from where we are meant to be, the path home is always open. It is never too late to realign with love and purpose.
- **In Buddhism,** the teaching of mindfulness encourages us to pause, reflect, and find peace in the present moment, even as we seek a new path.
- **In Hinduism,** the concept of *dharma* teaches that each person has a unique role to fulfill. Rediscovering your *dharma* is not about starting over but about uncovering the truth that has always been within you.

The Courage to Seek Your Joy

Finding your true joy requires courage. It asks you to step away from comfort, to question what you have been told, and to seek the place where your soul feels at home. This journey is not always easy, but it is deeply rewarding.

- **In Islam,** the principle of *niyyah* (intention) teaches that every step taken with sincerity and purpose is meaningful, even if the path is uncertain.
- **In Indigenous Spirituality,** the journey to discover your true place is often guided by vision quests or moments of solitude in nature, reminding you that your purpose is intertwined with the greater web of life.
- **In Satanism,** embracing individuality and rejecting societal expectations encourages followers to find their unique truth, living authentically and unapologetically.

Steps Toward Rediscovering Joy

1. **Reflect on What Brings You Alive:**
   o Ask yourself: *What moments make me lose track of time? What activities fill me with energy and peace?*
   o These reflections are clues to your true joy, pointing you toward the work and relationships that align with your soul.

2. **Explore Small Changes:**
   o If you cannot leave your current work or circumstances immediately, start by integrating small acts of joy into your daily life. This might mean carving out time for a passion project, connecting with others who inspire you, or approaching your tasks with a new perspective.

3. **Honor Your Journey:**
   o Remember that discovering joy is a process, not a destination. Each step you take brings you closer to the truth of who you are and what you are meant to contribute to the world.

Reflection: Finding Your True Joy

1. *What is one activity or moment in your life that brings you true joy? How can you create more space for it in your daily life?*
2. *If you feel disconnected from joy, what small steps can you take today to begin rediscovering it?*
3. *How does your faith or philosophy guide you to align your actions with your passions, creating a life filled with meaning and connection?*

Rediscovering Joy as a Reflection of One

True joy is not something we achieve; it is something we uncover. It is the natural state of being aligned with love, passion, and purpose. When we find our joy, we contribute to the infinite flow of existence, living as reflections of One. If you are not where you truly should be, take heart: the journey to joy is always open, always calling, and always worth pursuing.

When Work is No Longer Work

If we all truly found joy in something, the very concept of "work" would fade away. There would be no division between labor and leisure, no need to measure our efforts in monetary terms. Instead, life itself would become a flow of purpose and passion—a reflection of the infinite creativity within us.

- **In Indigenous Spirituality,** work is often seen as part of life's natural rhythm, deeply integrated with the cycles of nature. Hunting, gathering, farming, and crafting are not seen as separate from spiritual practice but as acts of gratitude and connection.
- **In Shinto,** reverence for the *kami* imbues daily tasks with sacredness, turning ordinary work into an offering of respect and gratitude.
- **In Buddhism,** mindful work is a way to cultivate presence and compassion, transforming even the simplest tasks into opportunities for enlightenment.

When we work with joy, love, and intention, we align with the truth of One, recognizing that our efforts are part of a greater whole.

Overcoming Barriers to Joy in Work

Finding joy in work is not always easy. Challenges, stress, and external pressures can cloud our sense of purpose. But even in difficult circumstances, it is possible to rediscover joy by:

1. **Reconnecting with Purpose:** Ask yourself, *"How does my work serve others? How does it reflect my values?"*
2. **Practicing Gratitude:** Focus on the positive aspects of your work—the connections you make, the skills you use, the impact you have.
3. **Infusing Passion:** Bring your unique talents and interests into your work, finding ways to make it more meaningful and fulfilling.

By shifting our perspective, we can transform even the most mundane tasks into opportunities for growth, connection, and contribution.

Reflection: Finding Joy in Your Life

1. *Think of a moment when you felt fully engaged and joyful in something you were doing, whether it was work, a hobby, or an act of service. What made that moment so fulfilling?*
2. *How can you bring more passion, intention, and love into your daily work, transforming it into a reflection of purpose?*
3. *What does your faith or philosophy teach about finding joy in life? How can those teachings guide you in aligning your actions with your values and passions?*

Living with Joy as a Reflection of One

When we find joy in what we do, we align with the essence of One. Our work becomes more than a task—it becomes a way to express love, connect with others, and contribute to the infinite flow of existence. By living with joy and intention, we dissolve the barriers between work and life, creating a world where every action reflects the sacred, and every moment is filled with purpose and passion.

Nurturing Relationships: Purpose Through Connection

Living with intention also means prioritizing our relationships, nurturing the bonds that sustain and uplift us. Purpose is found in the love we share with family, friends, and community, as these connections are reflections of the divine.

- **In Buddhism**, relationships are opportunities to practice compassion and mindfulness, deepening our understanding of interconnectedness.
- **In Shinto**, relationships with others and with nature are seen as sacred, with rituals and festivals fostering harmony and gratitude.
- **In Indigenous Spirituality**, the principle of reciprocity teaches that relationships—whether with people, animals, or the earth—are built on mutual care and respect.

When we nurture our relationships, we align with the truth of One, recognizing that the love and care we give to others enrich our own lives as well.

Purpose in the Everyday: Transforming the Mundane

Living with intention is not reserved for extraordinary moments; it is found in the ordinary rhythms of life. Purpose can be infused into daily acts, transforming them into reflections of love and unity:

- Preparing a meal with care, recognizing it as an act of nourishment for body and soul.
- Pausing to appreciate a sunrise, connecting with the divine beauty of the natural world.

- Offering a kind word or gesture to a stranger, creating a moment of connection.

These small, intentional acts remind us that purpose is not a destination but a way of being—a practice of aligning our lives with the greater whole.

Reflection: Living with Intention

1. Think of a moment when you acted with intention—whether through service, work, or connection. How did it feel to align your actions with your values?
2. What small steps can you take today to bring more intention into your life, making each moment a reflection of love and purpose?
3. How does your faith or philosophy guide you to live with intention? How can those teachings inspire you to find purpose in the everyday?

Living with Intention as a Reflection of One

When we live with intention, we align our actions with the essence of One. We serve others as expressions of love, find joy in our work as contributions to the greater good, and nurture relationships as reflections of the divine. Purpose is not about achieving perfection; it is about living each moment with care, connection, and intention, creating a life that honors the infinite unity that binds us all.

Reflection on Purpose

Purpose is the thread that weaves meaning into our lives, connecting our actions to something greater than ourselves. It is the way we express love, compassion, and unity in the world—a sacred gift that allows us to contribute to the infinite. Reflecting on purpose invites us to ask profound questions about who we are, why we are here, and how we can bring healing and connection to the world.

Purpose is not fixed or singular. It evolves as we grow, shaped by our experiences, beliefs, and relationships. It is not about perfection or achievement but about living intentionally, aligning our actions with our values, and reflecting the truth of One in all that we do.

Purpose as a Universal Calling

Across faiths and philosophies, purpose is seen as a universal calling:

- **In Christianity,** believers are called to serve as the hands and feet of Christ, living out their faith through acts of love and justice.
- **In Hinduism,** purpose is expressed as *dharma*, the unique duty or role each person is meant to fulfill in alignment with the cosmic order.
- **In Islam,** purpose is about living in submission to Allah's will, recognizing that every action can be an act of worship when done with intention and sincerity.
- **In Buddhism,** purpose is found in the pursuit of enlightenment, living with mindfulness, compassion, and balance.
- **In Indigenous Spirituality,** purpose is rooted in reciprocity, honoring one's role in the interconnected web of life and contributing to the well-being of future generations.

These teachings remind us that purpose is not just about what we do but how we live—with love, connection, and an awareness of our place within the greater whole.

Healing Division Through Purpose

At its deepest level, purpose is about healing—healing ourselves, healing our relationships, and healing the divisions that separate us from one another and the divine. To live with purpose is to answer the universal call to bring light into darkness, to build bridges where there are walls, and to create unity where there is division.

This healing does not require extraordinary acts. It begins in the small, everyday choices to live with love:

- Extending forgiveness to someone who has hurt you.
- Offering kindness to a stranger without expectation of return.
- Advocating for those who are marginalized or unheard.

Each of these acts, no matter how small, reflects the infinite truth of One: that we are all connected, and that our actions, guided by love, have the power to heal and transform.

Your One Task is to Cure

Purpose, at its core, is about connection. It is about recognizing that we are not separate but part of the same infinite whole. In this truth lies a profound invitation:

"Your One Task is to Cure."

This task is not confined to curing physical ailments but extends to healing the divisions that keep us apart—divisions within ourselves, within our communities, and within the world. It is a call to live with love and connection, to bring unity where there is fragmentation, and to reflect the divine essence of One in all that we do.

It is also a call to advance humanity and knowledge, to embrace the boundless potential of what we can achieve when we act together. It challenges us to transcend ego and fear, to break free from the illusions of separation, and to work not for individual gain but for the collective good. It invites us to create a world where pure love reigns—a love that knows no boundaries, no divisions, no conditions.

This task extends beyond human relationships to include the healing of the planet itself. It is a call to honor the earth as sacred, to recognize our responsibility as stewards of its resources, and to act with sustainability and unity in mind. It reminds us that our connection to the earth is not separate from our connection to one another, and that caring for the planet is an act of love and reverence for life itself.

This is not merely an abstract ideal; it is a call to action. It invites each of us to contribute to this healing, in whatever ways we can, through our choices, our work, and our relationships. Whether through small acts of kindness, efforts to protect the environment, or the pursuit of shared knowledge and understanding, this task calls us to act with intention and purpose, to embody the unity and love we wish to see in the world.

When we live with this purpose, our actions become sacred, and our lives become a testament to the infinite love that binds us together.

Reflection: Discovering Your Purpose

1. *What gives your life meaning? How do your values and passions guide your actions?*
2. *Think of a time when you felt deeply connected to your purpose. What did it feel like, and how did it shape your perspective on life?*
3. *How does your faith or philosophy guide you to live with intention, bringing healing and unity to yourself, others, and the world?*
4. *In what small ways can you begin to answer the call to "cure"—to heal, connect, and love without limits?*

Purpose as a Reflection of One

Living with purpose is not about achieving perfection but about aligning with love and connection. It is about recognizing that each of us has a role to play in the infinite whole, and that our actions, no matter how small, carry the power to transform. *"Your One Task is to Cure"* reminds us that we are not separate, that our purpose is woven into the fabric of existence, and that by living with love, we reflect the truth of One in every step we take.

Part VI: A Shared Journey

Life is a journey, not one we walk alone, but one we share with all of existence. Along this path, we encounter truths that transcend culture, language, and belief—truths that bind us together, reminding us that we are all part of something infinite. These shared truths are not just ideals to strive for; they are the essence of what it means to be human and the reflection of the divine within us.

Through love, compassion, unity, and purpose, we begin to see the eternal thread that connects us all. This thread is woven through every moment, every relationship, and every action. It is the story of One, the truth that we are not separate but deeply, inextricably connected.

1. The Eternal Thread

Reflecting on the shared truths explored throughout this journey reveals the eternal thread that runs through every tradition, every life, and every corner of existence. These truths are not bound by time or place; they are the foundations of life itself.

Love as the Essence of All Things

Love is the heartbeat of the universe, the force that gives life meaning and binds all creation together. Across every tradition, love is described not as a fleeting emotion but as the very fabric of existence:

- **In Christianity,** love is the essence of God: *"God is love."* (1 John 4:8)
- **In Buddhism,** love manifests as *metta* (loving-kindness), extending boundless care to all beings.

- **In Indigenous Spirituality,** love is reflected in the reciprocity of giving and receiving, honoring the interconnectedness of life.

Love is the eternal thread that reminds us we are never truly alone. It calls us to care for one another, to nurture the earth, and to see the divine spark in every being.

Compassion as the Way We Connect

Compassion is love in action. It is the bridge that spans divides, connecting hearts and healing wounds. Through compassion, we recognize the shared struggles and joys that unite us:

- **In Islam,** Allah's mercy inspires believers to extend care to all creatures.
- **In Judaism,** compassion is reflected in the teaching that saving one life is like saving the entire world.
- **In Taoism,** compassion is one of the three treasures, a practice that aligns us with the flow of the Tao.

Compassion is the way we see ourselves in others, the way we soften the edges of division, and the way we build a world where love and understanding prevail.

Unity as the Ultimate Realization

Unity is not about erasing differences but about embracing them as part of a greater whole. It is the recognition that beneath our diverse paths lies the same truth: We are One.

- **In Hinduism,** the Upanishads teach that *Atman* (the self) is not separate from *Brahman* (the universal reality): *"Tat Tvam Asi"* (Thou art That).
- **In Sikhism,** the principle of *Ik Onkar* declares the oneness of God and humanity, calling believers to see no distinctions between themselves and others.

- **In Modern Satanism,** individuality and critical thought contribute to the collective unity, reminding us that embracing diversity strengthens the whole.

Unity is the ultimate realization, the truth that all beings, all moments, and all elements of existence are threads in the same infinite tapestry.

Purpose as the Path We Walk

Purpose gives direction to our lives, guiding us to live with intention and meaning. It is the way we express love, compassion, and unity in the world. Purpose is not about achieving greatness but about aligning our actions with the greater whole.

- **In Buddhism,** the Eightfold Path offers a guide to living with mindfulness and balance, reflecting purpose in every step.
- **In Christianity,** believers are called to be God's handiwork, created to do good works that reflect divine love.
- **In Shinto,** purpose is found in honoring the *kami* and living in harmony with nature, celebrating the sacred in the everyday.

Purpose is the path we walk, the way we bring the eternal thread to life through our choices, actions, and relationships.

The Eternal Thread in Everyday Life

This thread is not abstract or distant; it is present in every moment of our lives. It is the love we show to a friend, the compassion we offer to a stranger, the unity we find in community, and the purpose we bring to our work and relationships.

- It is in the quiet moments of reflection, when we feel deeply connected to something greater.
- It is in the joy of creating, the fulfillment of serving, and the peace of simply being.

- It is in the realization that our lives, though seemingly small, are part of an infinite story—a story of connection, of healing, and of love.

Reflection: Seeing the Eternal Thread

1. *Think of a moment when you felt deeply connected to something larger than yourself. How did it change your perspective on life and purpose?*
2. *How can you bring love, compassion, unity, and purpose into your daily actions, weaving the eternal thread into everything you do?*
3. *What does your faith or philosophy teach about connection, and how can those teachings guide you to live as part of the greater whole?*

The Eternal Thread as a Reflection of One

The eternal thread is the truth of One: that we are not separate but deeply connected. Through love, compassion, unity, and purpose, we reflect this truth in our lives, creating a world that honors the infinite and celebrates the diversity within the whole. As we walk this shared journey, we are reminded that every step, every act, and every moment is part of something far greater than ourselves. I am One, You are One, We are One.

A Final Reflection

As this journey draws to a close, its truths remain only the beginning. The insights we've explored—love, compassion, unity, and purpose—are not just ideas to ponder but guiding lights to carry into our lives. These truths call us to live with intention, to act with kindness, and to embrace the infinite connections that bind us together. They are a reminder that the journey of One is not an abstract path but a lived reality, present in every thought, word, and action.

Carrying These Truths Forward

- **What if love was the language of your heart?**

Imagine if every interaction, every decision, every moment was rooted in love—not just for those close to you but for the stranger, the earth, and even yourself. How would this transform the way you see the world and your place within it?

- **What if compassion guided your steps?**

Consider how your daily life might change if compassion was the driving force behind your actions. How would you respond to challenges, conflicts, or opportunities to help? Compassion doesn't erase difficulty, but it opens the door to understanding and healing.

- **What if unity was the lens through which you saw the world?**

What if you saw every person, every being, every moment as part of the same infinite whole? Unity does not mean sameness; it means recognizing the sacred connection in our diversity. How would this shift the way you approach relationships, work, and your purpose?

- **What if your purpose was to live these truths every day?**

Purpose is not about grand achievements but about aligning your life with these truths—choosing love, practicing compassion, seeking unity, and living intentionally. Imagine what the world could be if we each embraced this as our purpose.

A Call to Live as One

This reflection is not just an invitation; it is a call to action. To love with courage. To act with compassion. To honor the unity that connects us. To live with purpose. These truths are not confined to the pages of this book—they are alive in the choices we make and the lives we touch.

We may walk different paths, but we are not separate. Each of us carries the infinite within us, a spark of the divine that unites us all. To live as One is to see this spark in ourselves and others, to let it guide us, and to let it light the way toward a world where love and unity prevail.

Reflection: Embracing the Truths

1. *What small step can you take today to make love, compassion, unity, and purpose part of your daily life?*
2. *How can you let these truths guide your interactions, your choices, and your journey?*
3. *What does it mean to you to live as One? How can you embody this in your relationships, your work, and your connection to the world?*

Walking Forward Together

As you step forward from this moment, remember that the journey of One is not walked alone. Every act of love, every moment of compassion, every choice to honor unity and purpose creates ripples that touch the lives of others. Together, we create a world where these truths are not just ideals but lived realities—a world where love is the language, compassion is the bridge, unity is the foundation, and purpose is the path.

Together, We Are One

God is One